7.95

THE SPIRAL OF LIFE

Unlocking Your Potential with Astrology

Joanne Wickenburg & Virginia Meyer

CRCS PUBLICATIONS
P.O. Box 20850
Reno, NV 89515
U.S.A.

Library of Congress Cataloging-in-Publication Data

Wickenburg, Joanne, 1944–
   The spiral of life.

   1. Astrology.   I. Meyer, Virginia, 1927–
II. Title.
BF1708.1.W52   1987   133.5   87-6567
ISBN 0-916360-00-8

INTERNATIONAL STANDARD BOOK NUMBER: 0-916360-00-8

Published simultaneously in the United States and Canada by:
CRCS Publications
Distributed in the United States and internationally by
CRCS Publications
(Write for current list of worldwide distributors.)
Cover Design: Image and lettering by Tony White.

This is a revised, expanded edition of *The Spiral of Life*, originally copy-
righted in 1974.

Contents

GUIDELINES FOR CHART INTERPRETATION

THE SPIRAL OF LIFE

Who Are You?
(The Spiral of Life)

1. (♈) Do you know who you are?
2. (♉) On what do you base your self-worth?
3. (♊) Are you learning from your daily experiences?

* * * * *

4. (♋) If the answers to these three questions are "yes," then you should be able to build stable personal foundations and a solid self-image.
5. (♌) Are you expressing your emotions through creative activity?
6. (♍) Are you willing to make personal adjustments to the world outside yourself by applying your knowledge in a practical way?

* * * * *

7. (♎) If so, you should be able to relate well on an interpersonal level and work harmoniously within equalitarian relationships.
8. (♏) Are you willing to control personal ego-centered desires out of respect for others in your life?
9. (♐) Are you trying to expand your knowledge, seeking a larger understanding of life through your social experiences? Can you see the broader viewpoint?

* * * * *

10. (♑) If so, you should be able to build solid foundations through which to operate on a social level, or gain a social image.
11. (♒) Are you searching for social or group awareness through shared expression and humanitarian experiences?
12. (♓) Are you willing to commit yourself to what you believe even though it may call for personal sacrifice?

* * * * *

Then you are ready for a startling experience . . .

There's a new life coming!!

1.

Getting It Together

People are looking for direction, integration and greater consciousness. "I wish I could get it together," they say. As astrologers, we know that understanding and living with the cosmic birth pattern is an exciting and trustworthy path to increased self-awareness and purposeful living.

To this end, a growing body of knowledge about astrology's relationship to psychology has become available from many sources. This new kind of interpretation is completely open-ended. Any student who can effectively use what is already available can go on to find more applications and insights. Most remarkable, however, is the phenomenon that happens when you learn how to integrate all these factors in your chart. You find yourself well on the road to integrating these same factors within your psyche. The occultists have always called astrology a "path," and Dane Rudhyar has likened the chart to a mandala, an archetypal symbol of the self. This path—this search for selfhood—is now open to modern individuals in a much less esoteric and more practical way. Whether you synthesize your own chart or have someone else do it for you, you may discover yourself walking that open-ended path to greater self-knowledge.

An important theme of this book is the SPIRAL development of life on several levels. Through the conscious use of the
spiral unfoldment of the chart (to be explained further in a
later chapter), we can develop our potentials in increasingly
deeper ways. The spiral effect concerns how we look at the
zodiac as a progression from one sign to the next in which the
growth of one sign appears to evolve out of the development
of the previous. Likewise, one complete cycle of the signs
develops into a new cycle which operates at a higher energy
level than the previous.

As one zodiacal cycle is completed in Pisces, a new one is
born in Aries . . . daily, monthly, yearly, or in a larger sense,
once in a lifetime. Simplistically, the spiral concept of the
zodiac is like the growth cycle of a plant. The seed sprouts,
takes root, blossoms and forms seeds for new growth before
dying. The seeds of our experiences, and the degree to which
they have been nurtured and utilized, determine the quality
of the next cycle. By understanding where you are now in
this process of unfoldment, and where you have come from,
you can approach the future more consciously and confi-
dently. Our purpose is to demonstrate how this spiral operates
in your life and how you can use it to intensify and enhance
your own growth process. (For a general example of how the
Spiral of Life progresses, refer to page 6.)

The question, of course, when using astrology as a path for
growth and self-knowledge, is how to "get it together"—the
chart, that is. A group of students were discussing the process
of chart interpretation and the following comments were over-
heard:

> ". . . I have ten books with descriptions of signs, houses, aspects,
> planets and two that give descriptions of planets in signs and
> houses, and planets in aspect to each other. But, I still get
> overwhelmed when I look at a total chart. I just don't know
> what to do with all that information."

> ". . . I think there are books that tell you what to do with the
> total chart, but they are so abstract that I can't understand
> them, let alone apply the information."

". . . They always suggest 'keys' to something intriguing and never say what they really mean. They don't tell you what to do with it. I know all those writers must know exactly what to do with their abstractions in an individual chart. I just don't know what they're saying."

We sympathize because we are still asking questions ourselves. It is hard to say why the subtle art of synthesis has not been explained in plain terms. Whatever the reason, it is time that the mushrooming materials available now to the student be organized into a form the mind can grasp. In the Aquarian age, knowledge belongs to everyone, and we can all be our own astrologers.

Science has demonstrated that the normal human psyche can only be aware of a total of about seven stimuli at any given moment. Naturally, when you look at 10 planets, 12 signs, 12 houses and their multiple relationships, you could feel overwhelmed if you believed you were supposed to see it as a "whole." However, this is not what understanding the chart as a totality is about. There are two ways to do it, as Dane Rudhyar has pointed out. One is to analyze each element of the chart individually, then try to see the total impression all the little steps leave in your mind. The other is to assess some of the overall patterns in the chart, such as chart type, balance of qualities and elements, balance of hemispheres, etc. Then proceed to the details, keeping in mind the larger picture as a framework. Both are necessary approaches. In our first volume we emphasized the latter approach and discussed the overall patterns in detail. We still feel this is a good approach, but realize that it is the organization of the individual elements that make interpretation difficult. It is these elements and their inter-relatedness that we hope to clarify in this book.

Our general approach is to present everything twice—once in outline or key-phrase form to show the organic structure, then in detailed form to fill out the meaning. Key-phrases for signs and houses will be found in *Your Cosmic Mirror*, the workbook supplement to this volume. (See the back of the

book for information on ordering it.) In-depth material on
signs and houses and planets are in the chapters on the signs in
this volume. Phases are presented in outline, then in detail, and
so on. The key to the organization of the material is found in
the Appendix at the back of the book. This is an outline showing an orderly procedure for focusing attention on all the important facets of interpreting a chart. Details of all the steps
and meanings are, of course, found throughout the book, but
the outline organizes these details—the contents of the chart—
so that you see them all in relationship, which is part of the
"over-all-ness."

By following the outline *after* you have digested the rest
of the book, you can be sure you have covered every important factor in a chart from the psychological point of view. If
you write out the first few charts following the outline, you
will soon discover that a total picture emerges out of the
detail, and at that point you will have grasped the meaning of
"chart synthesis." From then on, practice is your royal road
to success, and in time you will probably discard the outline
and use one of your own design. We do not intend to imply
that our book makes interpretation easy. There is no way to
do that. Furthermore, a thousand hours of reading books will
not make a student into a professional. Only sitting down and
going through the long arduous process of interpretation
many times will make you even reasonably efficient in "reading" a chart.

Since encompassing all the information between these
covers and getting it all down in outline form is still a rather
large task for a beginning astrology student, we have prepared
a separate workbook, *Your Cosmic Mirror*, which is a supplement to this volume. It contains sets of key-phrases as mentioned above, for the signs and houses. These are coded so
that you can use them in the appropriate places on the work-
sheet. These worksheets, one for each sign, using the key-
phrases, describe the signs in your own chart, the houses they
occupy, and how the rulers function in relation to the rest of
the chart, as well as the rulers of the houses themselves. In a
short while you can write out a "mini-analysis" of your whole

chart and see how rulerships work, as well as how the natural houses relate to their corresponding signs. Once you have done this, the next step of following the outline will be much clearer and easier.

2.

Toward Greater Consciousness

In *The Digested Astrologer*, Vol. I, we mentioned that everything starts on a psychological level in the house of Aries, and on a material level in the First House. This principle is behind the system of many astrologers who begin analyzing a chart with the Ascendant, the natural house corresponding to Aries. Since the planets represent the action connected with signs and houses, we can also use this system to go through the chart according to the planets in the order of the rulers of the signs: Mars (Aries), Venus (Taurus), Mercury (Gemini), Moon (Cancer), etc.

The logic of this approach can be seen in the development of a child into an adult. At an early age Mars urges us to initiate action based entirely on personal desire in order to prove our existence to ourselves. We then become aware of the material world as it relates very personally to us through possessions (Taurus/Venus). Then, we begin to intellectualize or perceive the connections between ourselves and the people of our environment as well as learning facts about the material world (Gemini/Mercury). As a result of the intelligent activity of moving out into the environment, we have to build personal foundations. We become aware of our need for security (Cancer/Moon).

As adults, we have learned in varying degrees to express our Mars urges within the framework of Saturn. By this time, we have reached more or less full self-consciousness (Leo/Sun) of being and action. It is the Sun which hopefully will offer the main key to the central motivations, vital energies, will-power and sense of direction behind Mars' activities. Because of this central significance of the Sun, we prefer to begin interpretation with it as a key to our total consciousness and a primary asset in life.

As the center of the Solar System, the Sun shines its light to each of the planets. This is symbolic of the consciousness which the natal astrological Sun brings to the various personality functions (planets) of the personal chart. We can see its life-sustaining energy in action through its yearly transits around the chart, revitalizing each of the natal planets as it conjuncts their degree. The Sun not only indicates the level of consciousness, but it also represents the *center of consciousness,* often called the "self." For people who have achieved a measure of the greater understanding represented by the 3rd fire sign, Sagittarius, the Sun represents the "Self" which is perhaps what religion calls the individualized "soul." By this, we mean that mature consciousness includes not only the conscious personality with its learned mechanisms and responses, but some kind of relationship between this and the unconscious side of the psyche.

While the Sun shows our awareness in the *present* (our total consciousness), it is also our source of power for progress or evolution into the future. The sun is the power of growth, integration and rebirth. However, without our daily experiences and the memory of past experiences to learn from, the unfoldment of consciousness could never come about. This is the function of the Moon in its monthly path around the Zodiac as it reflects the light of the Sun successively on all the areas and functions of our lives. Part of its face is in shadow which represents that part of our submerged unconscious selves which is readily available on demand or with a little effort.

To understand more about the role of the Moon, we can look at how the three water signs relate to the past, which underlies and supports the present. The past (which is always unconscious) is not only the matrix of all embryonic activity or the substance of whatever becomes conscious, but that which submerges, inundates and often destroys areas of consciousness that have become sterile in order that they might be reborn on another level.

CANCER is the familiar past of childhood and all that we have suppressed for some *reason* and therefore can call back out again.

SCORPIO is the deep past within the *sub*-conscious. Psychologists say it contains primordial memories and urges as well as very early traumatic childhood experiences or memories blotted out for reasons known only by the subconscious. Some say it contains the memories of past life experiences which have never been assimilated into consciousness. The dark side of the Moon may be related to this deep, hidden past.

PISCES is the higher unconscious or the "super-conscious" which is normally made available only to the Sun-consciousness when it willingly turns away from the personality awareness toward something larger. It seems to contain the sum total of all the wisdom we have gained from experience, but more than that, the inspirations of genius, universal love, spiritual at-one-ment. Psychologists have no satisfactory explanation for this side of the unconscious, although they are being forced to admit the reality of its presence.

Beyond all three of these areas of the personal unconscious is the vague, mysterious area called "the collective unconscious," containing the archetypes or universal patterns of perception and instinct. These hints of our ties to all of humanity from the beginning (whenever that was!) are reflected in and through the three personal areas of the unconscious. The Moon is the "imager" or imagination which brings them to consciousness in all the ways we mentioned earlier.

Because the Moon "reflects" the Sun's light and stores and controls the memories of the past, it contains images of all the forms known to us, out of which an infinite number of new images can be formed. "Invasions" from the collective unconscious are filtered through the personal unconscious and reflected in the conscious mind by the Moon, using images called up from the Cancer storehouse.

This substance of the past (personal and racial) underlies the present consciousness, the Sun, which is the sum total of our sense of being an individual. This self-consciousness has the power to rise up out of the past, reach toward something ahead (because it can think consciously) and eventually transcend the past. But it needs the Moon to do it, every step of the way. Conscious and unconscious are the two great polarities, the Yang and Yin of life, and the person who denies either one will be in a sense "destroyed by the other." Ultimately, they must be integrated if we are to achieve the process of *individuation* (Sagittarius) which is the step after *individualization* (Leo). At this point we refer you to "The Point of Illumination" in the section on Arabian Parts for a key to the integration of the two sides of consciousness. Also, see the section on the Moon's Nodes.

It is the Sun-oriented or Person-oriented astrology that people need today. We need these keys to some kind of direction and purpose which make sense out of a seemingly chaotic future. We need to find our selfhood, our awareness of the powers of the unconscious as well as the truly centered and necessary powers of the human conscious. The cosmic diagram—our birth chart—contains these keys and many more, if we can only learn to read them.

3.

The Planets

The planets represent the psychological functions of your personality. They show where the action is and are responsible for the actual drama of life. The Ascendant, although listed with the planets, is not an active function in the same sense. In Jungian terms, it is probably the "persona" and operates as a bridge or connecting link between the Sun's inner consciousness and the outer world. It can be seen as a kind of conditioning process whereby you learn how to relate to the world at the level of your true individuality.

THE SUN: ☉

The Sun represents the center of consciousness—which includes both the conscious and unconscious sides of the personality. Dane Rudhyar says it is the "am" of the "I am," and elsewhere he calls it "the power of the soul," but not the soul itself. It operates in the present and shows our potential for growth, will, decision-making, as well as creating the capacity to control and integrate all other elements of the chart (personality). The qualities of the

---

Note: The planets' phase relationships are mentioned in this chapter, but will be discussed in greater detail in Chapter 4.

Sun sign can be used to redirect the crystallized Moon patterns into paths more suitable for the present purpose (Sun).

THE MOON: ☾

The Moon represents emotional responses and habit patterns based on the stored images of past experience. It rules the first seven years of life, representing the past out of which all emotional responses arise. There are always some old habit patterns that are crystallized or too heavily structured and therefore no longer useful or growth-producing. The Moon is the focus for the Sun-consciousness.

THE ASCENDANT:

The Ascendant shows the basic way you make contact with the outside world. It represents the personal image through which the Sun, Moon and planets have to operate. The Sun, as the center of the personality, achieves *self*-consciousness through the Ascendant's experiences. The early childhood conditions (traditionally ruled by the first house) determine the type of experiences (sign on Ascendant) most likely to lead to the sense of "selfhood" and of being a separate individual. For this reason you often identify with the Ascendant characteristics and fail to see the direction of the Sun as the vital individualizing force behind the activity which characterizes selfhood. You then project a sense of separateness or self-ness to others, without the warmth of the Sun, the heart and the center of the personality. If you let the Sun operate through the Ascendant, you are able to reach a greater, deeper and more purposeful sense of selfhood.

In terms of the chart it is necessary to remember that all the functions, represented by planets, must operate through the Ascendant. From this point of view it is very revealing to check the distance and aspects of the Sun and planets from the Ascendant (refer to chapter on the first house). The relationship of the Sun in this case should reveal where you are in a cycle of conscious selfhood, self-awareness, self-direction and growth.

MERCURY: ☿

Mercury represents your ability to perceive, communicate,
make mental connections and classify knowledge. The sign
shows your manner of learning and communicating. It
shows your ability to intellectualize or understand your
emotional responses (Moon) and the ability to learn from
experience (Sun). It formulates and communicates the
Sun's will and purpose to the personality, in terms of the
Moon-images.

VENUS: ♀

While Mercury shows how you learn from experience,
Venus shows the values you develop due to these experiences. The sense of value evokes the power of love—the
most powerful magnetic energy in the world—an energy
which not only draws what you value to yourself, but
holds it there because you are finding meaning through
it. Venus focuses the effort to realize the meaning and
significance of the Sun's experience. If Venus is combust
(within three degrees of the Sun), that meaning is very
subjective and you are unaware of larger significances.

MARS: ♂

Mars is the ability to take action at any level of desire—
physical, emotional, mental or spiritual. All action is
preceded, however unconsciously, by an image of the
desired result, even at the level of taking one step after
another. This image is formed from the memories of past
experiences (Moon). You cannot form conscious images of
anything you have not previously experienced in some
form. Therefore, the relationship between the Moon and
Mars shows how this process operates.

The Mercury-mind provides the link which coordinates
the image and the physical response required to take
action. Venus represents the value behind the activity,
the meaning which inspires the desire. The phase relationship between Venus and Mars shows how these two
functions operate together. The Sun's function is to direct
the Martian energy toward a purpose or a goal. Mars is
therefore energizing the will (Sun) by putting it into action.

JUPITER: ♃

Mars, being the first planet beyond the Earth, represents the self going out to fulfill its desires and needs. Once you have confronted society in your effort to fulfill your personal wants, you discover you can expand more through cooperative action. Jupiter symbolizes the Sun-consciousness expanding through the broader knowledge gained from social contacts, such as friendships, education and religion. These contacts build a set of principles, morals and ethics as a foundation of social values that qualify the desires and actions of Mars as they build a broader viewpoint.

It is Mercury, of course, through which you learn and communicate in this wider experience. Its phase relationship to Jupiter shows this process operating in you, and how and where (position of the part of Mercury/Jupiter) you apply the knowledge gained from your experiences, thus maintaining your personal individuality among others.

SATURN: ♄

Saturn represents the place you build for yourself in society through Jupiter's cooperation process. Saturn begins by representing the authority (parental, social, inner) in your life which draws a boundary around all the inner planets by conditioning, defining and structuring their functions. It separates the conscious from the unconscious, individualizing the conscious personality (ego) and when it does this to the extent that it entirely blocks the unconscious, it separates people from others. Saturn should discipline and strengthen the Sun's will, developing character and responsibility. However, "you" as "Sun" should never identify entirely with this conscious self or ego, forgetting the values and needs of the unconscious side.

The phase relationship between the Moon and Saturn shows how Saturn (social conditioning) is structuring past emotional responses and habits. Saturn is responsible for these crystallizations. The Saturn conditioning defines the patterns of perception (Mercury), even at a very elementary level such as concepts of up and down, right and left or symmetrical patterns. It represents the particular kind of logic belonging to our culture. Therefore, the relationship between Mercury and Saturn will show how we use logic in our thinking and whether we are rigid or disciplined in our concepts and communications.

Venus, without the discipline of Saturn, can be expressed as self-centered love. Saturn forces you to define your values at a deeper, more socially responsible level. If Venus is square Saturn, you may in the past have "put boundaries around" your love expression or limited it "for the other person's own good." Now society or your conscience insists that you love certain people, and you feel unable or that it is unreciprocated. Your ego makes you try, but the effort *can* leave you full of resentment or guilt, and a sense of being unloved. On the other hand, in the best sense, the effort will lead you to a truly deeper expression of responsibility in love and a less selfish kind of affection.

URANUS: ♅

Up to a certain point we all identify a part of our Sun *consciousness* with the Saturn-conditioned *conscious* personality. This combination is "ego." We are in varying stages of releasing the *total* consciousness (the wholeness of the self) from the limitations imposed by this surface conscious awareness, although this limited awareness *has* been necessary to our development as individuals.

Through intuitive flashes of reality beyond the conditioned level (coming from Uranus), we become aware that we have greater potential than we were taught to believe. As we open up to this possibility we begin to tune in to universal truth, beauty and inspiration (coming from Neptune). Uranus operates through the mental levels of the personality, releasing our perceptions from their conditioning (Saturn) and allowing Jupiter to expand the Saturn boundaries. This enables more of the unconscious to be individualized or brought into the consciousness. Little by little the Sun-center becomes more unique, more all-inclusive.

NEPTUNE: ♆

Neptune represents the key to the experience of the wholeness, the oneness, the wisdom of the unconscious—personal, collective and transpersonal. Neptune can be experienced in art, music, poetry and all forms of created beauty, including the truly beautiful action of a person who commits himself to a high belief. You can see this quality in others, but to achieve it yourself calls for the same commitment. Such people responded to the transforming collective images of Uranus and allowed Neptune to dissolve some of their Saturn ego-boundaries. If you do not allow Neptune to dissolve the fragments of ego left over by Uranus, you will continually trip over them, falling into society's traps—the illusion of drugs, alcohol, glamor and all forms of escapism. You have to give up every thing personal that stands in the way of your commitment or it will be taken away. The commitment has to be for something larger than self and will be lived out by Pluto.

PLUTO: ♀

When Uranus cracks open the rigid walls of the conscious ego, you are invaded by the waters of the unconscious (Neptune). This includes ideals of life as it should be, but the remaining ego, inexperienced in dealing with the vastness of the unconscious, cannot discriminate between the real and unreal in the world he is living in and is overwhelmed by a longing he cannot put into form.

Pluto then takes over to organize the formless ideal or unconscious contents that have been projected into your life. It forces you to face some ultimate reality concerning your role in society in which you have to use that Neptune ideal or inspiration. If you do not use your commitment in total dedication to the Pluto role, the compulsive urges of Pluto will destroy the ideal, which remains only as an illusion that opens you to deception and eventual destruction.

4.

Phases of the Planets

Dane Rudhyar, in his book *The Lunation Cycle,** has brought to the attention of modern astrology the significance of the phase of Moon to Sun. 35,000 years ago, Moon phases were the center of early astrological religious and agricultural practices. In recent times, less attention has been paid to phases, and, in any case, the early meanings are of little value today unless reinterpreted. Thanks to Dane Rudhyar, the phases have been rediscovered in a new context, as the basis of personality functioning or expression.

There appears to be a direct relationship between the amount of shadow on the face of the Moon and the amount of consciousness present in the activity of the individual. We are not saying this has anything to do with the "level" or quality of consciousness. We are simply saying that some people function more readily from a basis of intuition or instinct and others operate more effectively in full awareness on the basis of past experiences (New Moon for the former, Full Moon for the latter). If an undeveloped quality of consciousness is present, the former may be subject to ego-projection, immature emotional responses and unreliable psychic activity. The latter

---

*Now available from Aurora Publications.

could be seeking fulfillment in something outside himself, based on a narrow and materialistic rationale. With developed consciousness, the New Moon individual is genuinely intuitive and idealistic, while the Full Moon person is making choices and relationships based on a conscious realization of meaning in his life.

For those interested in reincarnation, we do not imply that the Moon phase indicates a state of soul-development. If such an implication does exist, it can only be said with assurance that your Moon phase shows your development within a given cycle of manifestation. *It does not show the level of your cycle.*

The rationale behind phases is that the Moon-responses are conveyors of the Sun-consciousness. Like a lens, the habits, emotions and memories focus the consciousness, of whatever level, and express it in the things you give your attention to, the way you relate to others, the daily life in general. The more light the Moon reflects, the more consciousness it reflects, the more aware you are of all that has gone before and how it relates to the present. Therefore, the more capable you are of making decisions or laying plans on the basis of previous experience, and the more life requires you to do so. Furthermore, since the Sun represents direction and purpose in your life, and oppositions in general refer to awareness and fulfillment of purpose, the closer the Moon comes to the opposition of Full phase, the more aware you become of a realization of your own goals and a need to be a part of something larger. There should be, at the Full Moon, more of a reflection of that *total* awareness which the Sun as a personal center of consciousness represents.

This concept of phases is part of the philosophy of cyclic activity and behavior. It applies to any two planets in a chart, since all planets move at different speeds. In any given pair, one always completes an orbit before the other, beginning with a conjunction, reaching an opposition and returning to the conjunction. Any function of the personality (planet) is therefore related to every other function through the phase relationship. This is probably the most important key to chart synthesis in psychological interpretation. Once you have grasped the philosophic interrelationships of the functions as shown in the last chapter, you can use the phases to describe how these interrelationships are expressed in an individual chart. Then you will see vividly that while aspects show important emphases in charts, they are not necessary for an active relationship between planets. All an aspect shows is that two planets require some unusual effort in operating together, or, on the other hand, exhibit some unusual ease and productivity in doing so. When there is no aspect between two planets, it merely means that trying to operate these two functions together is not one of the bigger issues in the life. You will still use the planets together, and the phase shows the way you do it, in both cases.

The meanings given in the next section for the eight Moon phases can be applied to any two planets, but because we do not have space to describe every planet in phase with every other planet, you will find a section under the sign Aquarius where we have carried the Sun through the phases with Uranus, in detail, so that you can see how one goes about interpreting. Here are the basic key-phrases for the phases, and following that, you will find a very detailed section on aspects as they operate within phases.

The Eight Phases

NEW: Projecting an ideal or your ego. Plunging into new experiences and becoming a part of them.

CRESCENT: Struggling out of past conditions and dependencies which seem to hold on to you.

FIRST QUARTER: Changes being made in the environment in order to break out of past conditioning. Tearing down old structures and moving out to build new ones.

GIBBOUS: Analyzing previous self-expression to find a better technique through which to understand your personal part in relationships.

FULL: Thinking before you act in order to see the meaning in your actions and how your relationships are affected by them. Fulfilling some sense of purpose through others.

DISSEMINATING: Living out and sharing with others what you have found to be meaningful.

LAST QUARTER: Going through a traumatic psychological reorientation in order to allow something new to come into the old personal patterns of behavior or attitude.

BALSAMIC: Living out some new concept within old structures—commitment to the future, which brings transformation.

How To Find Phases

The Sun, Moon and planets always travel counterclockwise around the chart circle through the signs of the zodiac. The Moon travels faster than the Sun, so in about 28 days it will go from New Moon (conjunct the Sun) all the way around the chart and return to the Sun. It can never be more than 180 degrees from the Sun. It reaches this point exactly halfway around the chart, and this is called the Full Moon. When it is going through the first half of the cycle toward Full Moon, it is called *waxing*. When it is going from Full Moon back toward the Sun, it is called *waning*. During the entire cycle from conjunction to conjunction it goes through eight phases—New, Crescent, First Quarter, Gibbous, Full, Disseminating, Last Quarter and Balsamic. An easy way to find the phase between any two planets is to covert the signs into longitude. You will find a table giving the longitude equivalent of each sign on the following page under the "Phase Wheel."

IN THE TABLE OF LONGITUDES:
1. Find the longitude of the SLOWER moving planet and add the degree the planet occupies to that equivalent. (Jupiter at 3° Cancer = 90° + 3° or 93°.)

2. Repeat for the FASTER planet. (Mercury at 11° Virgo = 150° + 11° or 161°.)

3. If the FASTER planet is WAXING subtract the longitude of the SLOWER planet from the longitude of the FASTER. Locate this new degree on the *bottom* half of the Phase Wheel to determine the phase. If you cannot make the

Phase Wheel

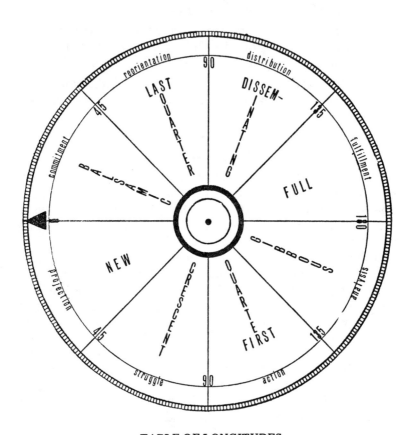

TABLE OF LONGITUDES

0° — Aries	120° — Leo	240° — Sagittarius
30° — Taurus	150° — Virgo	270° — Capricorn
60° — Gemini	180° — Libra	300° — Aquarius
90° — Cancer	210° — Scorpio	330° — Pisces

subtraction, add 360° to the FASTER planet. (161° - 93° = 68° or the crescent phase.)

4. If the FASTER planet is WANING subtract its longitude from that of the SLOWER moving planet. Locate this new degree on the *upper* half of the Phase Wheel to determine the phase. If you cannot make the subtraction, add 360° to the SLOWER planet.

5.

Phase-Aspect Relationships

Before beginning to interpret aspects in your chart, there are a few points of interest to be added. You will see that with each general phase description we have included a statement concerning a planet and its sign which is specifically related in meaning to that phase. The connection established between phase and planet is based on numerology and may only constitute one set of relationships since systems of numerology vary in their interpretation of numbers with astrological factors. This system appears to be meaningful and is the one currently in use. We recommend that you apply the planet-sign relationship only to Sun/Moon phases, even though the general descriptions of phases themselves apply to all planetary pairs. Otherwise, interpretation gets too involved, too subtle and finally meaningless.

When you are interpreting waxing phases and using the concept of "goals" or the search for meaning, you can look to the house, sign and degree that are opposite the placement of the slower planet to see, in abstract terms, what that goal might be. Using Dane Rudhyar's or Marc Edmund Jones' degree symbols may be meaningful to get further insight into the "goal." When you are interpreting waning phases and dealing with "something which fell apart" or with meanings that have already been established at the Full phase, the same procedure is useful. The degree on which the opposition point of the slower planet falls may often be meaningful to you in some very personal ways. If the degree symbol happens to be negative it may indicate that the "revelation or meaning" was an insight into how something ought *not* to have been. To learn from this experience can be valuable. On the other hand, during difficulties traceable to a planet in a waning phase, the degree of the former opposition point may give a clue as to what you should be doing about the situation—it could represent a "way out" of your difficulty.

THE WAXING HALF OF THE CYCLE: Action begins at an automatic, subjective level, primarily based on feelings and emotion, gradually developing conscious control as the phase nears the opposition. At the Full phase, the growing personal power seeks fulfillment in something outside itself, such as another person or an ideal or purpose.

As the distance widens between the two planets, up to the opposition, consciousness of one's relationship to the past, as well as the present, becomes more obvious. This creates conflicts between the past and the present, represented by the two planets. The slower planet represents a present pressure on the faster one to break out of conditions of the past shown by its house and sign. The faster planet is the function trying to get out of the past and establish something new in relation to the other.

THE WANING HALF OF THE CYCLE: Action takes place in full awareness of both past and present and of their contrast. Great tension is experienced as part of you wants to go one direction, part the other, until you feel "pulled apart." Action now needs to become deliberate and to have the purpose of finding an ideal within which both parts or activities can be integrated. The meaning of this ideal activity will be gradually released through the waning cycle, in terms of the progressed planets. "Group power" should replace personal power as your energies are spent in the release of significant meaning to others. If activity has been negative, patterns developed by the faster planet will crystallize and gradually disintegrate. Pressures from the slower planet are on the faster to reshape attitudes.

At any given stage of the total cycle, the *faster* planet represents activity. The *slower* planet represents the direction within which the faster is required to act. In some sense, the slower planet represents a directive from the present or future, while the faster shows by position and aspect something it is dealing with from the past, as far as its relationship with the slower planet is concerned. When there is an aspect between the two planets, the nature of the aspect shows the ease or difficulty in using the particular phase-energy available to them. It also shows that you are meant to emphasize these functions, attitudes and activities in your life.

THE NEW PHASE: In the new phase, awareness of the "past" has been blotted out. One therefore must go forward blindly toward some new experience instead of thinking action out beforehand on the basis of past experience. A residue of the past remains, however, in the unconscious (of early childhood? past lives? collective unconscious?). This residue comes out in the form of one's habitual responses and instinctual reactions where the faster planet is concerned. The slower planet is projecting its own meaning and sign quality through the faster, in order to get it started on the long road to building new patterns of activity based on more positive qualities of the sign. Naturally, if the slower planet (in any phase) is not operating well, the faster will not be "shaped" well, either.

When the Sun and Moon are in new phase, the whole personality is colored by the quality of instinctual activity, projecting either ego or idealism. If your personality is "new" you have a hard time being aware of your emotions or of why you do things. For example, if someone dies, you may berate yourself that you cannot experience great grief immediately. Later on (or perhaps when you see others express grief), you suddenly find your own and express it. The situation seemed "unreal," and so you had to see it outside yourself to realize it. If your responses bring negative reactions from others, you need to talk it out with someone who can point out to you what happened—then you (the Sun) "see" your own responses and can begin to change them.

THE SUN and LEO are associated with this phase, because people of this type have something to teach about self-expression and awareness. Leo people are experienced at self-awareness—they know what they are experiencing, how they are responding, and can control this to get what they want and to impress their personalities on their surroundings. If the new phase is important in your chart, some of the most significant people in your life will have strong Suns, Sun in Leo or many planets in Leo. The house governed by Leo in your own chart may be emphasized in some way.

♂ **Conjunction (0°)** — A focus of the two urges produces an emphasis on that combination and creates a power point. The faster planet is being forced to operate within the framework of the slower. This is a subjective activity, because the person is often completely unaware of the shaping effect going on. He is not very objective about himself, and his impulsive actions arise out of unconscious motivations. The closer the orb, the more likely this is to be the case.

⊻ **Semi-sextile (30°)** — There is a creative, productive potential, but some trial and error is needed to enable a planet of one sign polarity to project the quality of an opposite polarity smoothly. There may be some irritations to be experienced before activity is constructive.

Semi-quintile (36°) — The faster planet has the instinctive but often latent ability to project the quality of the slower planet in a productive and creative way. It may be no more than an inherent gracefulness in the functioning of the two planets, which is unconsciously projected and seen by others as something special about you.

Ν **Nonagen (40°)** — Inability to express unconscious elements in the house and sign of the faster planet are limiting the slower planet from expressing or projecting through it. Some "karmic" experience releases the material into the consciousness, bringing awareness that something from the past is clinging and holding you back. The house and sign of the faster planet describes what it is.

THE CRESCENT PHASE: The faster planet is struggling out of some past condition shown by its house, sign and aspects, in order to operate in tune with the slower planet. If the struggle is not successful, the faster planet remains in bondage to the past—with a deep, unconscious sense of being overwhelmed by it, or by "karma" or the "collective."

THE MOON and CANCER are associated with this phase. You need to build "forms" for the Sun's power. That is, where the Moon or the faster planet is you need to focus on activities of the house and develop clear "images" of the attitudes of the sign, so that the Sun or slower planet can accomplish its purpose through them. You can learn a great deal from your Cancer house experiences if your Moon phase is crescent because the faster planet is dependent on the past in some way, and does not really want to leave it. The Cancer house may show you something about that past.

∠ Semi-square (45°) — Your "projected" quality (faster planet) encounters a situation outside yourself which creates irritating mental tensions, mobilizing you to start struggling forward out of the past condition—economic (2nd house), educational (3rd house), etc.

S Septile (51°25') — In all phases it is important to remember that the conscious and unconscious have to operate together. At least, you have to take into account both sides of yourself and be aware of these needs. At the waxing septile, if your conscious patterns (faster planet) are dominating and ignoring the unconscious (slower planet), your unconscious will force situations that *make* you learn to be aware of the total self. This is why the septile is sometimes associated with compulsive and anti-social actions in which the unconscious is forcing itself on your attention. However, the unconscious can also be presenting you with hidden potentials in the house of the faster, through arousing responses in others to something in you of which you are not aware.

⁂ Sextile (60°) — Opportunity is available to move outward with a new quality defined by the slower planet and to produce something constructive with the faster in relation to it. This is a more active creativity than the trine because effort is needed to take advantage of the opportunities, and effort means energy is generated.

Q Quintile (72°) — There is a fully developed talent for calling on inner resources (related to the slower planet) to deal with conditions in the environment as shown by the faster. It may be latent, but if activated, it can transform the faster or recreate it in some sense so that it no longer needs to depend on the past for security.

THE FIRST QUARTER PHASE: At this phase you have a realization of dissatisfaction with the activity of the faster planet. Through forceful activity the slower is challenging the faster planet to tear down old structures and clear the way for establishing something new as shown by the slower. If activity is half-hearted or blocked, so is future fulfillment, because in this phase the potential for growth, revelation and integration is established for good or ill.

In this phase you *want* to change past conditions and take the initiative to do so, encountering resistance and crisis from those around you. This differs from the crescent in that there you are struggling with personal insecurities and afraid to let go of the past. Here you are struggling with those outside yourself.

JUPITER and SAGITTARIUS are associated with this phase because you are expanding your self-expression into your environment in order to establish it on a social level. Here, there may be ego-struggles. Crises in this phase are often due to ego-dominance. Jupiter, the urge to expand and improve one's consciousness, will give clues to the need for living up to your beliefs and ethics, not to your ego-demands. The

Sagittarius house may show an area where you really can expand with your growing self-expression.

☐ Square (90°) — The faster planet encounters a crisis in outer life due to attempts to live out a direction represented by the slower. The slower is trying to get you to build something new into your life, represented by the faster. Conditions compel you to take aggressive, sometimes organizing, action when structures of the past block the future goals of the slower planet.

△ Trine (120°) — Natural "vision" or talent makes it easy to build new qualities into the environment. A creative flow of energy can be released by the faster planet with little or no effort, in living out the direction of the slower. Joy of self-expression and out-picturing of ideas can be experienced. Doors open spontaneously. Your creative ability can change your surroundings.

THE GIBBOUS PHASE: You have the urge to contribute something of value outside yourself at the faster planet's position, defined by the goals of the slower. The goals are expressed in the opposition point of the slower. You are analyzing and eliminating non-essentials to perfect the personal expression of the faster planet. This is a preparation for aligning its activity with the goals of the slower and operating with others. You are searching for meaning, the "why" of what you are doing, because you are not fully aware of the slower planet's goals.

SATURN and CAPRICORN are associated with this phase. In this phase you have to learn better ways of functioning, which means building structures or patterns for the activity represented by the faster planet, based on the foundations of the slower. Here, you have to make contact with the past (Saturn) to find those foundations. Saturn, the father, society's accepted patterns, authorities, are all needed as some kind of example from which you can learn how to make your personal expressions more useful to others. Saturn shapes the boundaries of your activity in the world, and Capricorn shows where you are most likely to be accepted or rejected as part of the structure, based on your willingness to work within its limits. These areas of your chart cast light on your process of learning better techniques of expression, as well as your ability to discipline your unconscious reactions and your sense of responsibility toward others.

 Ϙ **Sesqui-square/sesquiquadrate (135°)** — There is a deliberate struggle in which you force issues to slowly clarify a goal. Problems in self-expression of the faster planet produce tensions making it necessary to eliminate unsatisfactory approaches. Discordant conditions based on your own abilities force you to analyze previous expression, which may lead to self-criticism and irritation due to difficulty in relating to others. This is a mobilizing aspect, as strong as the square in its own way.

 ± **Bi-quintile (144°)** — A developed analytical ability makes it easy to perfect yourself inwardly (faster planet) in terms of the slower planet's goals.

 ⊼ **Quincunx/inconjunct (150°)** — There is a need to develop outer techniques. Your faster planet's actual activity is not yet aligned with the goals of the slower. You may be pulling away from an old image or pattern established in the past, because it is not harmonious with those goals. Here, you have to consciously decide to go ahead and make necessary adjustments of the faster planet's function in the outer world, so it can operate in a larger situation in relation to others.

 ♂ **Opposition (180°)** — Ambivalence, indecision and instability result from the two parts of the personality pulling in the opposite direction. Sudden awareness of opposing circumstances due to outside conditions forces you to recognize the need to find ways of integrating the opposing activities.

THE FULL PHASE: There is a culmination *or* a falling apart of the two planetary functions as described by the need to relate the activities, and indecisions may develop concerning goals, meaning or purpose. This either breaks up the possible relationship or leads to the realization of larger overall structures within which both can operate meaningfully. The inner imbalance draws to you relationships that objectify your tension. These relationships are telling you that before acting through the faster planet you need to think to make sure your actions are meaningful. The part of your personality shown by the faster planet is operating strongly in relationships, and you have to consider others in what you are doing. Action should, at this point, be based on past experiences.

MERCURY, GEMINI and VIRGO are associated with this phase. The level of use of your concrete mind determines its success. If Gemini is more dominant in your chart it shows that you reach an intellectual realization of meaning and purpose. Its condition shows how you are able to bring conscious understanding of meaning into your actions, and that your involvement in the mental process is for the purpose of personal benefits and growth at some level. A dominant Virgo indicates an emphasis on getting your activity into efficient operation so that you can contribute meaning to something outside yourself.

♂ **Opposition (180°)** — A need develops to make this part of yourself (the faster planet) meaningful and think about the slower moving planet's purpose before you act, rather than operating instinctively. Plans not thoroughly laid will break up, or meaningless relationships fall apart. Revelation can come through maintaining open attitudes toward people around you in the house of the faster planet. Action here is meant to be based on past experiences.

⚻ **Quincunx/inconjunct (150°)** — You are reaching out from some kind of fulfillment or revelation in order to share it with others or live it out. *Or*, you are pulling away from something that fell apart, but have not yet found a direction. You need to consciously give up something personal concerning the faster planet in order to allow others to see what is meaningful to you. You need to find a direction and reach up to the fullest potentials defined by the slower planet. By hanging on to something you may be trying to control others through the faster planet's function. If this is the case, it will probably be taken away.

Bi-quintile (144°) — You can apply creative techniques in directing energies of the faster planet within relationships implied by its house position. Again, it may be latent.

THE DISSEMINATING PHASE: The faster planet shows how and where you can share with others or live out something that has been meaningful to you. The slower planet shows *what* it is that is meaningful. If you have nothing to share, that is exactly what you will be projecting, very verbally. People with Sun/Moon, Saturn/Moon, Mercury/Jupiter in this phase are obvious "communicators." Any two planets, however, in this phase imply some kind of out-going communication of meaning.

VENUS, TAURUS and LIBRA are associated with the disseminating phase. You have made something a meaningful part of your value system. You *value* what you are spreading to others. Also, something draws you toward other people, something that could be called love. Venus in the chart is, therefore, significant in showing where your values are focused. If Taurus is emphasized, you are disseminating for some kind of results —probably for your personal benefit (this need not be negative). If Libra is accented, you are doing it for others' benefit because you have really extended yourself.

    ⊡ **Sesqui-square/sesquiquadrate** (135°) — The faster planet is trying to express something that is meaningful in relation to the slower. The need to share is strong, but lack of proper control and direction may make you "come on too strong" and appear to "know it all," which is irritating to others. If activity has been negative, you may experience a sense of defeat in the house of the faster planet. It would be easy for you to lose yourself in something that allows you to forget your responsibilities.

    △ **Trine** (120°) — The slower planet enables the faster to share your ideas or ideals and convince others that they are meaningful. Others can see the vision and fully developed talent behind your actions and communications.

THE THIRD QUARTER PHASE (Last Quarter): Experiences you encounter with other people (through the slower

planet) make you aware of the need to reorient your own attitudes (faster). There can be a strong sense of disillusionment
with old values. The faster planet wears a mask in its area of
life while the change is going on. The mask is represented by
the old ways, which are rigid and "unreal" at times, as a projection for what is going on underneath. When you are ready
to live out the new approach, you drop the mask. The phase is
mainly reorientation of attitudes or values.

URANUS and AQUARIUS are associated with this phase.
Uranus has always represented bringing something new into
the old framework, at the idea level. Uranus shows how and
where you want to break out of some past patterns based on
what other people think. The Moon shows the old attitudes
that are being reoriented. Something about the Aquarius
house will show the results of the change. Transits of Saturn
to Uranus and Uranus to Saturn give clues to timing.

☐ Square (90°) — You experience an inner conflict between
   your old ways of relating to the outside world, and a
   strong urge to find new ones, which leads to the conscious awareness of the need for change. A decision has
   to be made. The slower planet seems to be demanding
   that the faster begin operating on another level, building
   new attitudes. Example: Mars square Venus—because you
   are initiating something new (Mars), you have to change
   your values (Venus).

Q Quintile (72°) — You are born with the ability to gain
   from society the assistance needed to make changes. The
   slower planet represents the assistance; the faster shows
   the area in which you make the change. Sometimes this
   ability is latent.

✳ Sextile (60°) — The faster planet finds opportunity to reorient itself easily to some new ideas defined by the
   slower. Activity in the house of the slower is helpful and
   meaningful to the faster planet's function, enabling it to
   produce something constructive or creative through the
   reorientation process.

§ Septile (51°25') — Some hidden wisdom connected with the slower planet reveals itself through others' responses at the point of the faster, and this experience reorients your attitudes. *Or,* antisocial attitudes force activity which causes society to "reform" you. Either way, you seem to be living out more than you are aware of in your present structures. The activities involved with these planets appear to be ruled by "destiny" or "fate," depending on whether they are operating positively or negatively.

THE BALSAMIC PHASE: Some new ideal has to emerge in the function of the faster planet, defined by the slower, even though that ideal can only be expressed within the framework of the present or the past. The new level of consciousness flows from the slower through the faster planet, transforming it. If you are blocking its transforming activity, something inside will seem to "die" or you will become confused. This phase is primarily one of transition, transformation or "seed-making." By "seed-making" we mean that this could represent a life of distilling your wisdom into some form that can be apprehended by others. This means that you are committed to giving something of yourself that others will take and build on and for which you, yourself, may be forgotten. Something truly does "die" here—some aspect of the ego.

We suggest that in the ephemeris you find the time previous to birth when the Sun and Moon (or two planets) in this phase were conjunct. The degree, sign and house of the conjunction will indicate the symbolic purpose of the experience of the two planets. Your job is to throw out what is not meaningful in larger-than-personal terms and condense what is left, as a "seed" of some new purpose in terms of the two functions. The sign and degree of the *coming* conjunction could give an abstract clue to this new purpose.

MARS and SCORPIO are associated with this phase. Mars represents instinct, Uranus intuition. Instinct derives from the collective unconscious, but intuition comes either from a source of greater truth or from a set of patterns relating to

the process of individuation (as opposed to "individualization"). For a person with a Balsamic Sun/Moon, Mars' relation
to Uranus is highly significant because the awareness of universal brotherhood has to transform personal desires (in-
stincts) to higher levels. In other words, to fulfill the Balsamic
purpose, personal desires have to be changed into group-
oriented desire or aspiration. (Pluto therefore also relates to
this phase.) MARS in this situation can represent a purifying
process. SCORPIO shows where hidden parts of the ego are
stored in the deep unconscious, needing to be released and
integrated into a more universalized personality. Mars shows
how this will be done. Pluto shows the new self that emerges.
Reading our section on "Aries Re-born" (Chap. 22) will be
useful here.

The point of all this seems to be that with unregenerated
ego-material existing in the unconscious, you are blocking
the flow of the new ideas or ideals which make it possible to
transform all your experiences into something meaningful to
those who will come after you. This does not apply only to
those gifted few who become famous after death for what
they have left to posterity. It applies to anyone at any level.
All Balsamic Moon people have something to leave behind
them of value, if only to one person.

∠ **Semi-square** (45°) — The slower planet creates irritating
mental conflicts with the faster, experienced at the latter's
position, which mobilize you to make a conscious break
from the past and let an awareness of something new start
operating through you. Irritations come from the fact that
the strong urge or idea has no new structures within which
to be expressed.

N **Nonagen** (40°) — This may represent a need to overcome
an attitude or feeling of being withdrawn or isolated by
letting go of some ego-factor (faster planet) and making a
definite commitment to the future on a different level
(shown by the slower). It may mean self-sacrifice, deep
awareness of humanitarian values, the need for meditation
or withdrawal into yourself to gain spiritual development.

The experience brought on by the slower releases some part of you from "bondage" to the past.

Semi-quintile (36°) — You consciously move inward to learn a technique for channeling new attitudes (slower planet) through the old structures (faster planet).

⊻ **Semi-sextile** (30°) — The new is actually flowing through the old structure, but it is irritating you. The faster planet needs to be transformed by the slower so that the two opposite polarities can function harmoniously. Trial and error and a little effort are needed to make this productive in rebuilding for a new beginning.

♂ **Conjunction** (0°) — There is an emphasis or focus on the two functions which can be experienced as emptiness and confusion *or* as a total commitment to something ahead which you are already starting to live out now with power. However, you are still operating within the former structures (the unchangeables with which you come into this life, such as physical characteristics, some kinds of social conditions, etc.). During this life, you should see a gradual transformation of the faster planet by the action of the slower.

6.

Arabian Parts

Arabian Parts are sensitive points in a chart, obtained by calculating the combined positions of any one or two planets and one or two angles or cusps. Some of these parts were originally called "ascendants" of the planets. These were calculated only with the Sun and Ascendant by adding the planet's longitude to that of the Ascendant and subtracting the longitude of the Sun.* The major Part was "Fortuna," the "Ascendant" of the Moon. Using its formula, one can discover a place on the chart which is related to the Moon or planet in the same way that the Ascendant is related to the Sun. This point becomes the natural field of expression for a planet as a reflection or extension of the Sun or self, the individual's own particular outlet for its energy.

Other parts were found by calculating combinations of two other planets and a given cusp, or two cusps and a given planet. These were called by such names as Part of Treachery, Part of Bondage, Part of Love, Part of Death, etc. Still other

---

*Note: Refer to the Table of Longitudes on p. 26 for a simple way to calculate these.

parts more commonly used now are called Parts of Expression. These consist of any two planets and the Ascendant, calculated by adding the faster planet to the Ascendant and subtracting the slower. Obviously, in the case of Mercury, Venus and the Moon with the Sun, these parts will also be the "ascendants" of the planets, since these three have faster orbits than the Sun.

Not all parts of expression will be "ascendants" of planets. The purpose of these parts of expression is to characterize the phase relationship between any two planets. They show where that combination is naturally expressed, or where the phase energy finds an *outlet* in this particular individual's personality. The sign shows the quality of expression. Frequently you will find that taking the time to calculate the part of expression will reveal a release for the problem in a chart where two planets are in waxing or waning square, and the individual is having difficulty handling the energies. The person may need to transfer his energies from one area of life to another, where he would find himself functioning more easily and naturally. Aspects to the parts are also significant, showing other functions that help or hinder expression.

To summarize we have:

A. ASCENDANTS of the PLANETS: (The Ascendant plus the planet minus the Sun.) These show the unique character of distribution of the planet's energy.

B. PARTS of EXPRESSION: (The Ascendant plus the faster planet minus the slower planet.) These characterize the phase relationship between the two planets and show where the combination is naturally expressed, or where the phase energy finds outlet.

C. SPECIALIZED PARTS: (Various combinations of house cusps and planets.) These mainly relate the planets to the material activities of the house in some way.

There are also Parts of Spirit. These are found by reversing the calculations of any part. For example, the original

Part of Spirit is found by reversing the formula for the part of fortune (Ascendant plus Sun minus Moon). The Part of Expression of Mercury/Jupiter is Ascendant plus Mercury minus Jupiter, while the Part of Spirit of these two planets is Ascendant plus Jupiter minus Mercury. There is considerable disagreement at present on the meanings of the Parts of Spirit. Traditional meanings are no longer adequate and sufficient research has not been done to warrant a statement at this time. However, we *do* feel one can use the Part of Spirit and have indicated below our method of interpreting it.

Dane Rudhyar describes a further sensitive point which he calls the Point of Illumination in *The Lunation Cycle*. This is always the degree exactly opposite the Part of Fortune. We refer you to his book for a detailed explanation. Our interpretation is below, based on his material.

Besides the basic parts we have listed below, which we find useful in in-depth chart analysis, we think you will find it useful to study the Part of Moon with every other planet in the chart, the Part of Saturn with Jupiter and Uranus and the Part of Pluto with Mars and the Sun. Wherever planets are in aspect and you are considering the phase relationship, the part will be useful. This is also true in all cases of planets representing polarities, i.e., Mars/Venus, Mercury/Jupiter, Saturn/Moon, Mercury/Neptune, etc.

The Meaning of Parts

The PART of FORTUNE: Here is the focus for the energy of the Sun/Moon phase. It represents the potential for developing the kind of personality described by the Moon Phase, and at the same time, it describes by sign the quality projected by the personality. The success of the Part of Fortune depends on the person's efforts. The search for happiness attributed to this part is really a search for freedom and power of self-expression. Aspects show what helps or hinders. (It's important to note that according to Rudhyar the Part of Fortune shows by sign your most natural way of releasing the energy of the New Moon before birth.) The house position of the Part of Fortune shows where, by instinctively nurturing an activity, you are actually helping the personality to develop.

The PART of SPIRIT: This is the index to your spiritual well-being, representing your implicit or inborn values. You are fulfilling the past in order to transcend it, and what you learn from the past in the area of this part can help you now to lead the Part of Fortune into a better level of expression.

The POINT of ILLUMINATION: Through this attitude (sign) and activity (house) you can gain a fully *conscious* expression of your Part of Fortune, which is normally instinctual. It is where you put meaning and content into the Part of Fortune and it could also be your spiritual path of illumination.

The PART of INDIVIDUALITY: (Asc. + Sun – Uranus) The part of expression of Sun/Uranus shows where you are consciously seeking to express your inner individuality. It is the sensitive point in your chart which characterizes the phase relationship between Sun and Uranus, showing your unique way of expressing its meaning in your own life. It shows the way you can expand your consciousness from a personal to a more universal level, and the area of life in which the expansion is carried on.

The PART of IMAGING: (Asc. + Uranus – Sun) The Ascendant of Uranus shows where inner individuality makes use of your conscious purpose and personality energies by sending you "images" or ideas from the unconscious. Experiences of the house draw them out to transform the personal ego into a more universal expression.

The PART of CONFRONTATION or RESPONSIBILITY: (Asc. + Saturn – Sun) The old "Part of Fate" shows where responsibilities to others from the past can no longer be avoided.

The PART of DEATH: (Asc. + cusp of 8th – Moon) This does not have anything to do with the death of the body except incidentally. It shows where old responses have to die and new ones be born. Naturally, under some circumstances, refusal to change could bring death to the body. We feel it is very subjective, a psychological point deserving some research. It might even show the psychological causes underlying one's final illness or cause of death, in some circumstances.

The PART of SELF-UNDOING: (Asc. + Neptune -Sun) Also called the Part of Treachery, this is where self-centeredness invites treachery or deception from others. Learning to face reality where this part falls and developing true concern for others makes this part a potential for spiritualization of the personal consciousness.

The PART of STATUS: (M.C. + Moon - Sun) Zipporah Dobyns is responsible for this one. It seems to represent an activity through which you instinctively seek recognition.

The PART of DESTINY: (M.C. + Sun - Moon) Dr. Dobyns is also credited with this one. It shows your life direction in terms of achievement at the social level.

The PART of SOUL: (Moon + 4th cusp - Sun) Our own discovery, showing how and where you are responding to your own personal realities.

The PART of COOPERATION: (Moon + 7th cusp - Sun) Also ours, showing your instinctive search for fulfillment through relationships.

Other Interesting Parts of Expression

To find these, just add the first planet to the Ascendant and subtract the second.

Sun/Pluto: How and where you can consciously express your sociological purpose or where your personal purpose can work together with your sociological role.

Pluto/Sun: How and where your God-self or your sociological potential is incorporated into personal purpose.

Pluto/Mars: How and where your unconscious urge to contribute to society transforms your personal drives and actions and desires.

Mercury/Neptune: How and where you sense and communicate ultimate ideals or meaning.

Venus/Neptune: How and where you share universal dreams, values and love in relationships or through talents.

Moon/Neptune: How and where your personal nurturing instinct operates at the universal level.

OTHER TRADITIONAL ARABIAN PARTS:

The Part of Love: (Asc. + Venus - Sun) How your values and love nature express your total consciousness.

The Part of Passion: (Asc. + Mars - Sun) How your energy and desires express your total consciousness.

The Part of Increase: (Asc. + Mars - Sun) Better called the Part of Expansion, it shows how your principles and social urge express your consciousness.

The Part of Bondage: (Asc. + Moon - dispositor of Moon) How you are bound to the past through the mask that you wear. Where you are projecting your bondage to the past.

The Part of Responsibility in Love: (Asc. + Saturn - Venus) How your responsibilities express your love.

The Part of Sickeness: (Asc. + Mars - Saturn) How your attitudes toward authority affect your actions and sense of responsibility. (Sickness is often the result of repressed aggressive drives.)

The Part of Karma: (Asc. + 12th cusp - ruler) Sometimes called the Part of Private Enemies, it shows how you are dealing with your karma in daily life.

The Part of Marriage: (Asc. + 7th cusp - Venus) How you merge your values and love-power with those of another person.

The Part of Divorce: (Asc. + Venus - 7th cusp) How your
values and love nature express your ability to relate. This
is only negative if not integrated.

7.

The Nodes

The Moon's Nodes mark the points where the Moon's orbit crosses the ecliptic or the Sun's path. The North Node is where it crosses going north and the South Node is where it crosses going south. They are always in opposition, and they operate in the same way as the opposition aspect. However, they are not functions of the personality, nor do they create activity in themselves. They are symbolic points of tension created by the Sun/Moon relationship.

The Moon represents past memories and habit patterns, many of which are no longer suitable to the purpose or growth represented by the Sun. For continued growth toward wholeness the old patterns have to be integrated into the total consciousness so that greater awareness can be developed. The Moon also represents the vehicle for the Sun's activity, and as you act, tension develops between the two nodes because your reactions oppose the Sun-purpose in some way or are unsuitable to its consciousness. Part of you wants to hang on to the past—a part conditioned by old social patterns. The house of the South Node will show the area of life most likely to draw you back into the older patterns. Another part of you is challenged to move forward into new experiences that widen your horizons. The house of the North Node shows activities that most often offer this challenge.

What you naturally and habitually do at the South Node tends to be automatic. These responses were learned so thoroughly and so long ago that they have dropped below the threshold of awareness. Because of this, the response becomes a "retreat," a "cop-out," an "ivory tower," a "line of least resistance"—all of which can be a drain on the psyche because they involve undirected activity.

The South Node activity will only take on personal meaning and direction if the experience of the house and sign of the North Node are actively developed. This draws the energy of the Sun-purpose and direction into that house to meet the challenge of the new, increasing the total consciousness. Then, the South Node energy release is continually replenished by new ideas, meaning, potential and purpose.

The shape of the South Node can be seen as an empty cup being filled by the upturned pitcher of the North Node.

$$\text{☋ N}$$
$$\text{☋ S}$$

When the challenge of the N.N. is ignored, anxiety or fear is connected with the S.N. Your "cup" is being drained and you are not refilling it with the fresh experiences offered by the N.N. The past on which you have become so dependent is being taken away, no future is being prepared to replace it, and you feel lost in the middle of a dry desert with no source of water. This is an appropriate symbol since dependence on the past is an emotional characteristic, and water is the symbol of emotion and the past.

On the other hand, if you focus all your attention on the N.N. and withdraw from all S.N. experience, the water will become backed up and stagnant, representing repressed energies or urges, psychological blocks, complexes, etc. Eventually the cup overflows, and the undirected energies and emotions flood the consciousness. Your identity becomes lost in collective attitudes, emotions, compulsions, and you are no longer able to know yourself as a whole person.

The message of the Nodes is that you need *both* the individual consciousness and the contact with the collective. You need both to grow as an individual at the North Node and to give that new individuality back to the collective at the South. If you don't keep growing as an individual you soon have nothing to give. If you refuse to give when you *have* something to give, it is *taken* away.

THE NODES and the MOON PHASE: The tension of all oppositions brings awareness. The Moon cycle as a whole symbolizes growth in consciousness. The tension between the two nodal houses indicates the direction in which such growth should take place. They show the opposites in your life which can bring the most awareness, from whatever point (Moon-phase) you are beginning. Now we can begin to put together all the vital factors connected with the Moon phase—the Nodes, the Part of Fortune and the Point of Illumination.

THE PHASE: The Sun shows your ever-new direction and purpose. The Moon represents past responses that conflict with that purpose to some degree, regardless of ease of aspect. The phase shows how the Sun's present consciousness is trying to reshape the past.

THE PART OF FORTUNE: This shows the unique way in which your Moon's emotions and responses express your Sun's consciousness and purpose. The success (a word often associated with the Part of Fortuna) depends on the degree to which you have allowed your responses to be reshaped by the Sun. You are searching for fulfillment, happiness and self-expression here, and the answers are very clear in every chart.

THE POINT OF ILLUMINATION: This house and sign brings meaning and significance that leads to greater fulfillment because you become aware of a purpose within which to express yourself (Fortuna).

THE NODES: As your Sun/Moon functions (according to phase) and expresses itself (according to Fortuna) tension is created between the houses of the Nodes. This is important to keep in mind at all times, because the inevitable tensions of the Nodes can always be traced right back to the Sun-Moon relationship. Nothing in a chart is ever unrelated to anything else, and the main purpose of this volume is to show *how* everything is related. As you objectively look at the tension in your own chart, and intellectually analyze the reasons, you are well on the way to being able to integrate those tensions within your own psyche.

THE NODES IN ASPECT TO PLANETS: A planet conjunct one of the Nodes is pulled into the tensions between them. If it is conjunct the South Node the natural urge is to emphasize the activity of that function. There is usually some well-developed natural ability in this function, but when used without the polarity of the North Node, it can be a fragmenting activity, stifling growth through getting caught up in collective patterns, such as seeking success without remaining in touch with the deep needs of your inner self.

A planet conjunct the North Node, while probably easier to deal with, can create its own problem. By adding its energy to the personal end of the polarity, it opposes or *withdraws* energy from the collective or the release end. Many people in this situation are afraid to enter into the experience of the South Node, resulting in the stagnant emotions mentioned earlier.

Planets conjunct the South Node draw people from the past into your life. These relationships will be draining (according to the house and sign meaning), not because there was necessarily anything wrong with the original relationship, but because they are not what you need *now* for growth. However, they cannot do you any harm as long as you are accepting the challenge of the North Node. They *can* help you find ways of giving out the assimilated results of what you learned at the North Node. A good example of this is the reformed criminal who is confronted by his old companions. He can be drawn back into his old ways or he can help them in a rehabilitation program. Planets conjunct the North Node draw people to you who make you grow and learn to see things in a new light, but you must share what you have learned with others or use it actively in your own life.

Planets square the Nodes create conflicts because the Nodal tension puts pressure on that planet, so that it is pulled two directions at once, which makes integration more difficult. Planets trine one Node and sextile to the other are functions that can be helpful in integrating the Nodal polarity. The dispositor of the North Node represents a function and activity (planet and house) which are necessary for the activation of the growth potential of the North Node. The dispositor of the South Node is a function and activity which is necessary in releasing the South Node experience.

8.

Eclipses

We believe that eclipses have, above all, a spiritual implication. Astrologers have associated them with disaster, but only because people generally in the past have not been able to relate to the planetary scope of the energies. Although it is not the purpose of this volume to go into spiritual astrology, some discussion is necessary and will be useful, because in our time people are becoming aware at a deeper level of their relationship to the Earth.

Dane Rudhyar wrote that at the New Moon (Solar) Eclipse, the future (Sun) is blotted out by the past (Moon), while at the Full Moon (Lunar) Eclipse, the past (Moon) is obscured by the present (Earth). This means, to us, that at each eclipse (Solar or Lunar) some of the Earth's karma is being symbolically activated. During a Solar eclipse, everything is obscured by the darkness of the Moon-shadow (past or karma), and we are forced to live out a new expression of an old, unsolved problem, gradually bringing it into our conscious awareness. It is important to remember that during a Solar eclipse, the dark side of the Moon is being illuminated by the Sun. Could this mean that the dark side of the soul must be confronted and integrated into our consciousness? At a Lunar Eclipse, awareness of our past is symbolically destroyed (the Earth blots out the Moon's light), and we are forced to incorporate our ways of living into a larger purpose or be, ourselves, burned out by the purpose we refused to see.

As the diagram below indicates, at the New Moon Eclipse (which is always a Solar Eclipse) the dark side of the Moon is taking the full force of the Sun's rays because the Moon is between the Sun and the Earth and in direct line with both. At the Full Moon Eclipse (which is always a Lunar Eclipse) the lighted side of the Moon is obscured by the Earth's shadow, since the Earth is now between the Moon and Sun.

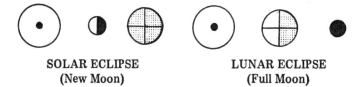

SOLAR ECLIPSE   LUNAR ECLIPSE
(New Moon)   (Full Moon)

THE NEW MOON ECLIPSE: We have already said that we think the dark side of the Moon represents the contents of a deeper unconscious, which is closely connected with the collective unconscious and racial memories, but which up to this point has not been revealed or is not a part of our experiences. Symbolically, the New Moon eclipse would suggest that the light of the Self is illuminating something of collective significance from the past to be lived out or projected instinctively in our lives.

In terms of the birth chart, a New Moon eclipse may show an individual whose responsibilities to the collective seem to take over the personal life. The personal destiny is eclipsed, and therefore he may feel that his own personal needs are submerged in larger demands. The person born under a New Moon eclipse cannot pursue personal goals other than within the collective need. If he tries to live solely for himself, he is "blinded" and does not have inner guidance for personal direction. His own selfish responses and goals will meet with disaster. In a dark place he has taken a wrong turn.

If this is you, you need to accept your larger role (Pluto) and life in a manner from which others can benefit. Pluto may be the key to your chart, and we recommend you analyze its place in your personality, as well as its transiting and natal aspects to the eclipse point. We are speaking here of anybody whose New Moon before birth was an eclipse as well.

In an eclipse-oriented chart, the Jupiter/Saturn phase is of unusual importance. It shows how you are operating in society as a separate individual, and it describes not only your place within society, but the significance that you put into that place. (For additional information we refer you to *New Mansions for New Men* by Dan Rudhyar, pages 129-137.)

The PROGRESSED NEW MOON ECLIPSE operates in a similar way. It shows a time in your life when your goals take on the significance of something more collective than personal. It may show a time when you can temporarily be released from past burdens or "debts" in order to take on a larger responsibility. Even though you are not aware of the deeper significance at the time, a contribution of a larger nature has been conceived.

As the progressed Moon increases in light the personal consciousness creeps into the picture. The Sun is gradually illuminating the old selfish patterns that were put aside at the conjunction, from whose hold you now need to struggle (crescent). The consciousness increases as the Moon progresses from New to Full. Illumination of the purpose behind the New Moon experiences is experienced. Therefore, the Crescent Phase introduces an extremely critical point in the cycle which will determine whether or not you are able to break out of the personal structures of the past or whether they will simply collapse with nothing new to take their place at the First Quarter square.

The "fateful" character attributed to eclipses is negative on the material level only if the person is unwilling to accept the death of the self-centered ego, because this kind of "death" will occur whether the person chooses it or not. Even the person who *does* meet this spiritual challenge will feel it was due to "fate" or that his life is fatefully bound up in some larger-than-personal destiny.

The FULL MOON ECLIPSE: At the Full Moon eclipse you are forced to operate at full consciousness, yet you no longer can call on past experiences, emotions and memories for understanding your purpose and direction. You need full contact with the "Self" which gives you awareness at a much truer level of reality.

In the light of the Sun, the Earth is casting its full shadow (the past or karma) on everything around you. You must now integrate this "collective past" into a personal purpose. Normally a Full Moon personality is able to use his own past personal experiences (at any point in his life) to realize personal fulfillment in something outside himself. The Lunar-eclipsed individual cannot do this because he is trying to find a more transpersonal place in the world than a merely personal past can sustain. He has to find meaning in his cultural, social, historical, religious past.

If you allow the shadows of either your personal past or the collective past to become so large that they engulf you, you never find fulfillment. You will be torn apart all your life until you are able to become more conscious and integrate the shadow of the past. Otherwise, you will project your shadow on others, causing physical and emotional separations in relationships. In the words of Carl Jung, concerning invasions of the conscious by the unconscious shadow:

> "It is really a state of ECLIPSE of CONSCIOUSNESS where people . . . do perfectly crazy things. . . . That could be a pathological case, but fantasies of this kind can also occur within the limits of the normal. I have heard innocent people say, 'I could cut him limb from limb' . . . When these fantasies get vivid and people are afraid of themselves, you speak of invasion."*

Analytical Psychology: Its Theory & Practice, by C. G. Jung, 1968, Pantheon Books, a division of Random House, page 34.

If you decide to turn toward the Sun with a larger, more total awareness, you may still experience separations, but ultimately these will represent *releases* from a personal past which allow you more fully to enter into a universal kind of experience. The PROGRESSED FULL MOON ECLIPSE operates in a similar way, showing a time in your life when this collective purpose begins to transform your personal purpose.

9.

The Spiral of Life

In *The Digested Astrologer*, Vol. I, we showed an aspect of the spiral development of life in the way one sign leads to the next, and one house underlies the experiences of the following house. We can go one step further and show how each sign not only describes the attitudes and needs of the house it rules but can lead to the further development of its corresponding natural house. In turn, each house contributes to the development of its corresponding sign in the natural chart. This simple, obvious fact has often been ignored, but by considering its activity in your chart, you will open new avenues for conscious growth in a progressive series of steps—even without considering transits and progressions.

In reading through the chapters on Signs, Planets and Houses we suggest you consider the following relationships between signs and the natural houses. Developing the quality of the sign leads to improvement of the natural corresponding house, according to the sign on its cusp. At the same time, pursuing the activities of the house, according to its ruling sign, contributes to the quality and level of the corresponding natural sign. This is the "spiral of life" in which each adds to the other's growth.

On this page we give brief key phrases to demonstrate half of this concept, leaving it to you to reverse the statements to see the circular effect. The workbook, *Your Cosmic Mirror*, contains more extensive demonstration of the principle which you can apply to your own chart.

Spiral of Signs and Houses

♈ Identity awareness and initiating new activity contribute to . . .   (1) self-image

♉ Productivity and building personal values contribute to . . .   (2) personal resources and a stronger sense of self-worth

♊ Associations and the ability to use reason contribute to . . .   (3) knowledge

♋ Emotional security contributes to . . .   (4) personal foundations

♌ Self-expression contributes to . . .   (5) creative activity

♍ Self-analysis contributes to . . .   (6) personal adjustments

♎ Awareness of others contributes to . . .   (7) cooperative relationships

♏ Deep involvements contribute to . . .   (8) joint resources

♐ Wider contacts contribute to . . .   (9) broader viewpoints

♑ Social identity contributes to . . .   (10) social foundations and reputation

♒ Social awareness contributes to . . .   (11) group goals and social alliances

♓ Commitment based on openness to higher realities contributes to . . .   (12) overcoming the past

10.
Aries, Mars,
& the 1st House

Aries represents the need to become a more well-defined individual. It is that part of you which is always in the process of becoming self-aware. Naturally, because you are an adult and part of a long train of cultural development, you are a conscious individual to some degree. Many people are very self-aware, while others are much less so.

In the beginning, children are not aware of their true separateness, but become increasingly so as they grow older and move out to prove themselves through their courageous feats. However, there are always parts of ourselves which have never been brought under conscious control so that we could express them with awareness, as well as just instinctually. We are always children, growing as long as we live, as far as our psyches are concerned.

The sign Aries symbolizes the emergence or birth of consciousness or separateness out of the collective consciousness (Pisces). The only way collective consciousness can operate in a person is through instinctual activity—action based on unconscious motivations. This impulsive action "happens," and over a period of time you begin to "see" it happening and to find some of the unconscious motivations, making them conscious. Because all instinctual activity belongs to and is conditioned by the collective memories, the act of bringing it into consciousness or under conscious control is an act of separating it from collective ideals and attitudes and making it a part of your own individual psyche.

This is why so many strongly Arien types are described with an emphasis on their *individuality*. An Aries Sun's main growth potential lies in his ability to become a separate individual to the extent he is able. Yet, he can become so hung up on individuality that he forgets he is still connected with the larger web of humanity. He may unconsciously manipulate and dominate others in his urge to "do his own thing" and to demonstrate his individuality. Yet it is his own basic insecurity as an individual which causes him to do so.

Because consciousness is mental, and Aries is an action-oriented sign, the Aries personality needs to *act* on ideas in order to see them consciously. This is why he may insist that you follow his ideas over your own, but also why when functioning at a high level, he really *can* take the lead in terms of ideas. This is where the key-words "pioneer," "leader," etc. come from.

The HOUSE of Aries shows that exciting place where instinctual activity, freely operating, gives you the opportunity to become more conscious—to add to your development as a separate entity. However, it is where, if you do not want to become separa*tive*, you need to be aware of others so that you do not diminish their individuality through your own dominance. This house is where you can be very creative, acting on the creative energies that lie below the level of awareness (Pluto). The exhilaration of these energies flowing through you here can make you feel that you really are in contact with the vital forces in your own personality which you define as "I AM."

In the Aries house, you need freedom to express new ideas and start new activities, to assert yourself (within reason), because you are trying to prove your individuality not only to others but to yourself. You are not concerned with planning ahead, which detracts from spontaneity, nor with the results that might occur. You are concerned only with action itself, the mirror on which you can "see" what has previously been submerged.

At its best, the resulting independence gives you a sense of individual identity, of courage, inspiration and creativity. Aries on the 4th house, for example (always difficult to interpret), indicates the need to bring into awareness those taken-for-granted feelings that form your emotional foundations. As long as they are identified with collective ideals and therefore unconscious, you are unable to feel secure within yourself as an individual. Aries on the 4th house suggests that no home or cultural background or tradition provides you strength you can depend upon. Therefore, you have to make conscious and individualize the inner resources existing in the collective consciousness. By doing so, you make them your own, which gives you courage and enhances your sense of identity. Involvement in activities which allow the symbols of selfhood, God-in-the-depths, centeredness, etc., to flow through you in the form of creative ideas is a way for you to reveal these inner resources. You may do this as a creative activity in your home, but it could be in any place where you feel in touch with your inner self.

PLANETS in Aries will show personality functions that need the new experiences available in the Aries house in order to fulfill the needs of the houses they rule.

SUN IN ARIES: The central purpose of your personality is shaped and developed through the self-initiating activity of the Aries house. The "ego" must become more aware of itself, prove itself, through the new activity initiated in the Aries house in order to operate with power and purposefulness in the house of Leo.

MOON IN ARIES: The emotional security sought in the Cancer house is determined by your ability to respond instinctively to the stimuli of the Aries activity. You need to move out courageously if these emotional needs are to be met. Crystallized habit patterns can make this response dogmatic and domineering if the Sun-consciousness is not expressed. Instinctive adaptation is required at a high level here.

MERCURY IN ARIES: The mental faculties are developed through your ability to create new ideas. You need to prove your identity through acting on these ideas. The future-oriented, pioneering, independent attitudes operating here determine the degree of fulfillment in the Gemini and Virgo houses.

VENUS IN ARIES: You instinctively draw new values from the collective consciousness and move out to prove those values in order to make them a conscious part of yourself, unique in terms of your own individuality. Your tendency may be to rush out and "love anyone" immediately, or try to force your values on others. The new values and people you draw to yourself here, at their best, fulfill the needs of the Taurus and Libra ruled houses.

MARS IN ARIES: Because Mars rules Aries, you fulfill your Aries needs right in its own house. The Aries individualism shows in your actions loud and clear as they are expressed boldly in their own natural sign, the sign of action. But lacking the "seasoning" quality of Mars in later signs, your actions may not bring so much consciousness.

JUPITER IN ARIES: Your progressive, self-initiated drive to move out aggressively and expand your realm of social influence and to widen your life philosophy fills the needs of your Sagittarius house.

SATURN IN ARIES: Your ability to build structures and to define your identity in the Aries house determines the level and degree of recognition received in your Capricorn house, as well as the stability and quality of your social image.

URANUS IN ARIES: The ability to express your own uniqueness instinctively needs the pioneering spirit and new activities of the Aries house in order to fulfill the needs of the Aquarius house. Spontaneous activity in the Aries house is

heightened by the presence of intuition and the awareness of the potentials of any situation.

IN THE 20TH CENTURY, NEPTUNE AND PLUTO WILL
NOT BE FOUND IN ARIES. While many individuals recognize and respond to the transforming influences of these two
outer planets, perhaps humanity as a *whole* is not yet ready to
live out the next phase of the spiral represented by these
planets.

MARS represents the personality function which initiates
all action and therefore fuels the identity (Aries). All action
is based on desire. (You have to want something before you
will reach out to take it.) And desire is an instinctual reaching
out to prove ourselves. Mars represents, then, the desire nature,
and its house position will show where your desires are most
strongly focused, as well as *what* it is you desire. The sign
describes the way in which you go out to get what you want.
Planets in aspect to Mars will define any obstacles or conflicts, as well as functions and areas of life which assist in
establishing identity needs. Example: Mars in Taurus in the
3rd house has a desire nature that is somewhat materialistic
because of the need to get results, and this operates in the
area of communication. You want to prove to others that
your ideas are worthwhile, productive and practical, so you
communicate aggressively. While Aries is the emergence of
conscious identity, Mars is the function of the identity which
reaches out, gaining new experiences and getting something
needed to *activate* the identity. Mars acts upon the need to
start something new, and these actions ultimately stimulate
growth in consciousness by giving form to unconscious urges.

IF MARS IS RETROGRADE, something in your early
life has prevented the normal flow of desire energy and has
held back your ability to prove yourself. Aspects to Mars,
and its dispositor, may give clues. This experience internalized
your energy so that the Aries house activity is directed more
inward and shared less with others until you have rebuilt your
basis for action in the Mars house. There is often an urge to
turn desire energies inward to discover one's own motives.
Freud had Mars retrograde, which was the key to his interest

in psychoanalysis. In any case, activities of the retrograde Mars house will offer opportunities to discover or get in touch with motivations, by the very fact that you often seem to do certain things over and over again until you understand why.

In addition to Mars, we feel the planet Pluto is also strongly related to the Aries identity. Although Pluto's effect on the Scorpio house is too strong to deny its rulership, we have found that the regenerative experience of Scorpio leads to a reborn identity, a living out of a more group-oriented desire nature in Aries. Please see the section "Aries—I Am Reborn" for further information.

THE FIRST HOUSE characterizes the nature of your self-awareness and shows where you physically emerge into a material world. The sign describes the experiences which lead most directly to self-growth and awareness. You identify with these kind of experiences and "see yourself" as this kind of person. The sign becomes a kind of role you play—sometimes called the "mask of the soul" and sometimes the "persona." Because the first house emerges out of the 12th house (related to the collective or society-as-a-whole) and indicates your early childhood conditioning, the sign on the first house is a conditioned or structured quality which describes your most natural and instinctive style for relating to the outside world.

If you see yourself in this role, you are obviously projecting this quality out to others. In fact, they see more of this than you do, and growth and fuller self-awareness come through the feedback of the 7th house, where you may be projecting negative qualities of the rising sign onto others. Due to this feedback you can perfect your personality through finding deeper significance and a larger purpose for what you are projecting, or the role you are playing.

The ruler of the Ascendant shows, by house and sign, the experiences necessary to develop self-awareness. If the ruler of the Ascendant is *intercepted*, you must quietly do the activities of its house in order to develop your outer personality. After you have grown in experience in the area of this

house, you may be able to bring the quality of the intercepted sign and planet out into the open. (For more information on intercepted signs and planets, see the section "A New
Life Coming.")

Continually starting activity in the Aries house contributes
to the growth in self-awareness in the first house. It should be
noted that the new Aries activity always has to be initiated
within the framework of your *Ascendant* attitude and approach. Even the sign quality of Mars operates within the
rising sign. In other words, all attitudes and functions of the
chart are filtered through the Ascendant, which is the basic
approach to life situations.

ASPECTS TO THE ASCENDANT show qualities other
people see in you as being more personally a part of what you
project. All planets ultimately have to "project" through the
Ascendant, but those in aspect do so much more strongly and
with more consciousness or self-awareness. Dan Rudhyar has
specifically emphasized the relationship of the Sun to the
Ascendant by phase as well as aspect. For more information,
see the section on the planets. Also, refer to the chapter on
phase-aspects for detailed descriptions of aspects.

CONJUNCTION: The conjunction is particularly strong because the function of the planet is "right there" where
others are seeing it most strongly. You tend to identify
with the function, as it is being projected outward as part
of your "mask." For example, Venus conjunct the Ascendant shows a person who projects his *values* outwardly
to others. He may *identify* with his own "beauty" or may
project something beautiful by living out his values where
others can see them in operation.

SEXTILE/TRINE: A planet in either of these aspects is a
function of your personality which you naturally and
easily incorporate into your contact with the world, and
project harmoniously to others.

SQUARE: A planet squaring the ascendant challenges your
personal identity by projecting a quality that is inharmoni-
ous with your rising sign or natural approach to life. It

is saying "you need to change the way you have been projecting me or you will get caught up in my negativity." What you project will distract you from true selfhood. It often seems easier to use the negativity of the aspect in order to get recognition, pity, sympathy, etc., from others. However, if you reorient the motivations behind what you are projecting (4th house square), or alter the quality of the outer life experiences (10th house square), you will find the opportunity to constructively use the energy of this aspect.

OPPOSITION: When a planet is in opposition to the ascendant, you see the 7th house qualities of yourself brought out and objectified through the people with whom you are closely associated. By its opposite nature, this planet will challenge the personal image you are projecting, defined by the rising sign. This challenge can bring about greater self-awareness and the potential for integration. If there are unresolved negative qualities in the rising sign, they may be projected on to the people you meet through 7th house experiences. Carl Jung states that projection is one of the most difficult of all unconscious activities to detect in your own personality. The only way you can find out if you are doing this is to check the impressions you are getting from others with objective data about them. If your relationships are arousing reactions that are beyond your conscious control, or if the people you draw into your life appear to be negative, take a good look at yourself and get an objective opinion about why this is happening. If you have problems in relationships, the ruler of the 7th house may show that "why." If you are projecting unconscious personality factors onto someone else, the ruler of the first house may show why. The planets that are in the 7th house indicate needs that must be fulfilled through relationships. The *kinds* of needs will be shown by the houses that these planets rule, and the needs will be objectified by the persons to whom you are relating.

11.

Taurus, Venus, & the 2nd House

Taurus, the farmer of the zodiac, represents Aries' outrushing psychic energies harnessed to the plough. Taurus values the results of Aries action and understands what steps and how many are required in achieving them because this sign has an inborn sense of the natural process behind any productive activity. This is why Taurus has such amazing capacity for carrying through to the finish. It is also the reason for the passiveness or laziness of the negative Taurus, who sees how much work will be involved and is reluctant to embark on the project. The emphasis may be on the enjoyment of some kind of results in the Taurus house instead of on the productive activity.

The second sign deals with the emotional need to possess something you can enjoy with the senses, which may be either the five normal ones or some higher kinds of sensing. This is why Taurus is the most sensuous sign of the zodiac. The need to possess and enjoy can drive you with a fixed determination to be productive and practical in the things of its house in order to produce tangible results that can be experienced in this way.

Here, the Aries identity takes root. In your Taurus house you find the results of the action you initiated in Aries. The main concern of its house is: of what use are these people or things to me? This may be very selfish or it may arise out of the realization that the meaning of experience or activity depends on its having a useful purpose at some level. When Taurus is not completely materialistic, it senses intuitively the greater purpose and rhythms behind what is seen on the surface.

Coming so closely after Aries, Taurus still contains a great deal of instinctive or unconsciously inspired action and is dependent upon the quality of the Aries ideas for its results. On a general level, this productivity is material or physical in nature, but if the Aries energy represents highly developed creativity, the Taurus results will be in the form of artistic or social expression, and what is done may have aesthetic or spiritual implications behind its practicality.

VENUS represents the function of the personality concerned with your ability to build material and personal values, based on the experiences you gained from Mars. The values you build determine what it is that you love and appreciate. Love is the attractive power you have within yourself to draw to you what you want to enjoy or to use in the Taurus house. From another point of view, Venus is the focus for efforts at realizing the meaning and significance of what you are doing in the Sun's house. The ability to appreciate, as well as the level of your values, stand behind the way you (the Sun) direct and integrate all the personality functions. (A solid understanding of these kinds of interrelationships of the planets leads not only to ease in synthesizing a chart, but in integrating your own personality and activities toward a unified purpose. See Chapter 3 on the planets for more details.)

Venus' house position shows what it is you most value and appreciate. The Venus love-power is often like magnetism, not only attracting you to others, but making you attractive to them. (See the chapter on Libra for more on this side of Venus.) Generally Venus in connection with Taurus refers to the material and physical, be it food, procreation, possessions or the physical expression of something artistic. In its relationship to Libra, Venus refers more specifically to interpersonal values based on your relationships. By sign and aspect, Venus will show the nature of your attractive power, and its house shows the kind of experiences you value and attract to yourself.

WHEN VENUS IS RETROGRADE at birth, you are revising the values of your Taurus house to a higher level. The inner feelings resulting from the experiences of the Venus house subconsciously stimulate changes in attitude toward possessions and enjoyment of the personal, material or physical world. Due to the re-evaluation process, some difficulty is experienced in the outward expression of your values, feelings, appreciation and love in the Venus house, which delays the fulfillment of the Taurus satisfactions.

MARS and VENUS together represent your creative energies. Sexuality, artistic creativity, the ability to release energy through play or "recreation" are ways of reproducing your Aries identity in the material world. The phase relationship between these two planets shows how this Yang/Yin energy operates. The part shows the area of life through which you most naturally release the energies.

The Aries house is where you need to prove yourself through the aggressive action of Mars. The Taurus house is where you need to get results and to enjoy the outcome of the Mars experience. The Victorian Age proved that repressing Mars/Venus urges caused nothing but psychological problems. On the other hand, the new era of free love is already proving that unrestricted expression becomes either boring, exhausting or unfulfilling due to lack of emotional involvement. Some psychologists are saying that the significance of this phenomenon is an evolving need to apply the sexual or reproductive energies to creative or cultural achievement.

Whenever Venus is in a *waning* phase to Mars it seems rather certain that the activity of these energies needs to express more *meaning* than personal satisfaction. The part shows the area of activity where the "meaning" could be found most easily. If such a person is having major conflicts relating to his sexual life, he is probably not applying these energies in that area. If Mars and Venus are *waxing*, the personal satisfaction is predominant. This means either the energies are meant to be used in developing your own personal sense of sexuality or your own creative expression at any level. The descriptions in this chapter of the eight phases of Mars and Venus show briefly the way your desires make you define your values, how your aggressive actions work in rhythm with your passive, receptive side. They show how you move out to get what you value.

However, what you want (Mars) is not always harmonious with your values (Venus). That's when Mars, through the results of the activity it initiates, makes you build stronger values. If Mars is strong and Venus is weak, the desires may operate with little regard for the values. Here you would find a strong potential for sex without love or meaning and appreciation for the partner. Or, it might show up in the inability to really enjoy the sensuous values as much. If Venus is stronger, the person's receptivity or love nature would be strong, but the ability to take the initiative in a love relationship is weaker. This may be the person who uses the reproductive urge in creative activity other than sex.

Some of the balance of Mars and Venus depends on whether you are a male or a female. Mars in a woman's chart represents part of the submerged unconscious side of her nature simply because she is a female body, and her hormones are in different balance than those within the male body. Therefore, a woman responds especially to a man described by the sign of her Mars, because he brings out or objectifies these qualities in herself. A man will respond especially to a woman answering to the description of his Venus sign position because his receptive side is partially submerged, and she will bring it out or objectify it for him. Also, up until recently, society has very actively conditioned males to repress their female side—gentleness, love of music and arts, intuition, etc.—and females to repress their masculine side—drive for identity, achievement, creativity, intellectual autonomy, etc. For these reasons, the aspects Mars and Venus make in a chart will have different significance and weight in male and female charts.

The PHASE of Venus to Mars operates as follows:

NEW: Your values operate instinctively through your aggressive drives. You are probably spontaneous in your sex life and project your sexuality magnetically. On a creative level, you are expressing your values unconsciously through the activity.

CRESCENT: The activity you initiate (whether sexual or creative) forces you to struggle out of past values connected with the Venus house. In order to be receptive you feel dependent on something in this house. However, Mars forces you to give it up because those old values cannot operate in the here and now.

FIRST QUARTER: Mars has forced Venus to break away from past values because they were no longer adequate for the present needs. Your new values as you live them out meet challenges from others that force you to build structures for them to operate in. Mars (desire) keeps forcing your Venus out to do it. Your love life will, therefore, be full of crises and change.

GIBBOUS: You are searching for techniques at all levels, sexual and creative. Your actions are leading you to the awareness that you need to perfect your values, and you are questioning your expression to develop better personal techniques.

FULL: Your sex life is unstable until you find deeper meaning in your relationships, which includes the needs and values of the other person. You are torn between your values and your desires until you learn to consciously direct your actions on the basis of past experience.

DISSEMINATING: In order to make your values meaningful you need to live them out. Your relationships are based on this desire to disseminate meaning and value through the expression of love. You need to find a partner who objectifies your conscious ideal. At a sexual level you are ready to have a meaningful relationship and share ideals with that person *or* you may simply be a "disseminating" sexual partner to many people because you selfishly think you are God's gift to the opposite sex.

LAST QUARTER: You go through an inner crisis over your relationships or previous sexual desires because you have outgrown your values and new ones are coming to life inside. Until you are sure of these new values you continue with the same approach to your Mars experiences, all the while aware that they are becoming more meaningless because they were learned and not truly yours at all. A sexual relationship alone is no longer filling your needs. You need to give and receive respect as a person and at a more conscious level.

BALSAMIC: You live out a new set of values with which society is not in tune. You make a commitment to these values, which later may be lived out openly by many people. If you find a partner with a similar desire-value system, you can have a satisfying and meaningful relationship but it will be unusual in some way, ranging all the way from highly idealistic to socially unacceptable.

   If you cannot find this ideal partner it may be a signal that you need to sublimate sexual energy into creative activity. Even if you do find a similar partner, you will need to find other levels of expression to some degree. Basically this phase seems to show a need to bring together the male-female polarity within your own nature as well as in relationships. Therefore, this phase can sometimes indicate the mystic or occultist who achieves "mystical union" or a deliberate and conscious use of sexual energies for spiritual purposes. Negatively this can extend to the black arts where sex is used to reach the astral planes.

THE SECOND HOUSE is traditionally associated with money and personal possessions. Psychologically, this interpretation is inadequate. The second house also contains inner resources, such as talents, as well as the substances of the body. The "substance" needed for second house activities may be material, but often is emotional or mental. All these resources (outer or inner) are the assets with which you cope with life. You can draw on whatever has been accumulated here to deal with all life situations. These assets comprise your sense of self-worth, self-esteem, self-reliance. This is truly your "house of values"—the value you place on yourself.

The sign on the second house defines what you need in order to build your self-worth, or upon what it is based, as well as your material possessions. It shows how you handle your assets. The ruler shows where you are able to fulfill these sign needs and build "substances" for yourself *without* depending on another person to do it for you. Oppositions between the second and eighth houses (or between their rulers) emphasize the importance of standing on your own two feet, even though you have to balance this material independence by sharing assets with others to achieve a larger purpose. And, as a matter of fact, your values and possessions become more meaningful when united with those of others. Nevertheless, it is important, even if you are dependent on a spouse, parent, etc., to develop the assets of the second house. This is true not only because at some time in your life you may find yourself alone and "on your own," but also because it is in developing your personal resources and talents that you realize your own worth.

12.

Gemini, Mercury, & the 3rd House

Gemini is concerned with awareness of the principle of duality, of Yang/Yin, Masculine/Feminine, Day/Night and so forth—all that is expressed in the form of opposites. (This can be seen in the house of Gemini, where you are concerned with understanding how your Aries and Taurus experiences are related.) Since everything in the knowable world is based on duality, Gemini is interested in everything! The house of Gemini shows where, motivated by curiosity and mental needs, you become personally involved in a variety of activities, contacts and associations which increase your knowledge. You are involved in so many experiences here that you find it necessary to classify them. You need to put them into some kind of intellectual framework that you can understand, in order not to be overwhelmed by the complexity of life. At one level you may simply become very clever with words and use them to gain your own ends. What you say may be based only on a large mass of experiences or factual knowledge. Gemini is the sign that can prove black is white if necessary. Some Gemini types communicate indiscriminately, without regard for the listener's need to hear, for the purpose of building up their own personalities. No wonder Gemini has been called shallow!

Yet, there is another side of Gemini that few recognize. The power of words is the single most important influence in our lives today, and the positive Gemini not only has the exact word for everything, but also is aware of the influence it will have on others and his responsibility in using it. It may not even be *words* that the Gemini is using. James Hansen, a Northwest sculptor, with a strong Gemini chart, communicates intellectual concepts from the deep past of mankind through the work of his hands. (Mercury rules the hands and arms.) These concepts have a strong emotional impact which, as with all mythical material, can never be completely put into words. It is interesting to note that some of the basic dualities which Gemini connotes are conscious-and-unconscious, mind-and-emotion, thinking-and-feeling. Spiritually, the evolved Gemini brings these together in some form such as the successful scuplture, poem, novel, etc. People who persist beyond the surface meaning of their Gemini house experiences will discover symbols and deeper significance coming from the unconscious, which contribute to their power of communication.

Gemini represents a stage in which all things have to be known in the light of what one already understands, and the family (symbolized by Cancer) represents symbolically "the circle of the known." Negative Geminis, caught in the duality of good and evil, project all sorts of unconscious darkness on the family. In an attempt to protect family security, they may erect many intellectual structures and forms—called by some "tabus." "You can only do this. You can't do that. This is good. That is evil."

How does your house of Gemini relate to your house of Cancer? Do you make of your Gemini experiences a rigid intellectual framework to put around your Cancer experiences so that the free-flowing emotional life of Cancer is dammed up behind the walls of the mind? Psychology warns us that if we protect ourselves too strongly from our own unconscious, our instinctual nature, by staying rigidly "conscious" and logical, the unconscious will come out in the form complexes and uncontrollable reactions. All signs have their particular forms of disease, and Gemini's neurosis is the use of logic as a defense against the unconscious, while this sign's complex is a projection—a spirit, a devil, a guide or something that goes bump in the night.

MERCURY rules the concrete mind, which deals with facts. It is the ability to perceive relationships of all kinds—in things, people or ideas—and to analyze, classify and store all such information it gathers in the process. The house of Gemini shows where the perception of relationships is most important in your life, and therefore where you need a variety of experiences. Being able to see how things or people are *alike* not only adds to your storehouse of knowledge, in terms of building concepts, but can help you find greater self-understanding. Mercury's sign and house show where and how this capacity for perception is shaped and developed. Your ability to use logic and reason here determines your capacity to communicate, make various associations and to understand the experiences of the Gemini house.

Mercury symbolizes the ability of the concrete mind to perceive whatever comes through the senses, sending the image to the brain, where it is stored in the memory (Moon). Much of the way we perceive anything is preconditioned by the society we live in and even the stage of collective psychological evolution. According to recent research, even the concepts of "up, down, horizontal, vertical" are preconditioned at very early stages of infancy. The ability to perceive things in perspective appears to have been nearly absent in the Middle Ages, according to what we find in paintings from that period. In all the more advanced and complicated mental processes, the same preconditioning persists. Saturn's relationship to Mercury shows something about the kind of limits being placed on your ability to perceive and think. Saturn focuses your perceptions in given areas until you learn to use those experiences in a conscious way.

Saturn builds the boundaries between the conscious and unconscious. Our parental and social conditioning tells us what things we can remember or even accept through conscious perceptions. Therefore, Saturn in the chart will give some clue as to the way in which Mercury can get material from the Moon's storehouse of memories. Hard aspects could show blocks and limitations in perception due to crystallized attitudes. Easy aspects could show access to the unconscious, but a conscious control is kept over the material brought out. The phase relationship, of course, is important between Mercury/ Moon and Mercury/Saturn as it shows the natural flow of energy between conscious and unconscious and the way the mental structures operate.

The sign VIRGO symbolizes another side of the Mercury mind which is actually inseparable from the Gemini perception side. That is the capacity to analyze the experiences and relationships which the mind stores and classifies, in order to decide which are useful and which need to be eliminated for greater efficiency. This also has a determining effect on what is conscious and what is unconscious. What is not going to be used immediately is dropped into the unconscious areas of the brain ruled by the Moon. In most cases, the computer-brain or librarian aspect of Mercury (Virgo) can find it when called upon to do so. In other cases, Saturn has censored and withheld it. In still other cases the unconscious planets have trapped it somewhere in the deeper unconscious. Many of these possibilities can be seen in the aspect of Mercury to Saturn and to the unconscious planets. These aspects will show your openness to material flowing not only from the personal unconscious but from the collective consciousness, as well as how social influences may block or control the natural flow between the two.

This is the great key to wholeness, according to Jung. The ability to remain conscious and at the same time be aware of the unconscious and open to its messages is necessary for mental health. This is the goal of the Mercury process—of the messenger of the gods who wants to relate the world of the senses and the world of the soul. This significance of Mercury to the evolving personality has never been fully appreciated nor explained by traditional astrology.

It now becomes clear that such combinations as Moon in Gemini, Mercury in Cancer or the 4th house, Moon aspecting Mercury, Moon in the 3rd house, etc., help to bring together the two sides of our total consciousness—the logical and the irrational. With these combinations, there is also always the need to avoid emotional thinking, over-intellectualization of the emotions, and lack of concentration. On the other hand, the nurturing qualities of water make the mental processes fruitful and productive.

MERCURY RETROGRADE will be covered in detail under the section on Virgo, since Virgo becomes the prime influence when Mercury is in this condition. Likewise, in the following descriptions of Mercury's relationship to all the planets, we have skipped the relationship to the Sun. It will be covered under Virgo, since the Sun is a significant part of the retrograde function. We have already described the relationship to the Moon, which is defined by Mercury. All other planets define Mercury, so we will now look at the way the mind is affected by the other personality functions.

VENUS/MERCURY: The Venus urge for relationships and its sense of values determine the kinds of associations you make, how you communicate and the knowledge you gain. Because you have values, you want to understand the significance of relationships. Your relationships shape your communication ability.

Example: Venus in Gemini in the 7th, Mercury in Aries in the 4th. The values you gain through intellectual relationships shape the way you build independent intellectual foundations for these relationships.

Example: Venus in Cancer in the 7th, Mercury in Gemini in the 5th. The values you gain through warm, close, human relationships shape your creative or romantic communications.

MARS/MERCURY: Your ability to move out and act independently as an individual shapes your courage in communicating your own ideas.

Example: Mars in Taurus in 10th, Mercury in Libra in 3rd. Your drive for practical achievement in the outside world shapes your urge toward an intellectual, possibly artistic, type of communication.

JUPITER/MERCURY: The capacity to expand your life through participation in group life shapes your ability to communicate your individuality to others.

Example: Jupiter in Pisces in 3rd, Mercury in Scorpio in 11th. Your urge for mental expansion through commitment to an ideal defines your ability to perceive deeply and communicate the goals of the group.

URANUS/MERCURY: Your intuition, inventiveness and ability to see beyond the limitations of what has been structured by society shapes your ability to release your mind and perceptions from preconditioned patterns long enough to bring something new into the conscious mind. In aspect this can make you erratic or a genius.

NEPTUNE/MERCURY: The wisdom you have gained from accumulated experience and from contact with deep, collective images from the unconscious which allow you to see the wholeness of life, defines your ability to see basic facts in a larger context. In aspect, it gives you the ability to synthesize complex combinations or it creates confusion.

Example: Neptune in Leo in 8th, Mercury in Aquarius in 2nd. The way you sacrifice ego-centeredness in dealing with others' resources shapes your ability to use your unique intellectual resources for coping with life and supporting yourself materially.

PLUTO/MERCURY: Your contact with the deepest personal unconscious and the images of the collective unconscious determines the degree to which you consciously relate to society in its largest sense. In aspect, they make you adept at research, political propaganda, psychiatry or the ministry, or else you compulsively communicate emotions that have been repressed for a long time.

Example: Pluto in Cancer in 8th, Mercury in Taurus in 6th. Your ability to allow relationships to release and transform deeply hidden, self-centered emotional energies shapes the powers of communication that you bring to your daily work or personal services.

THE THIRD HOUSE represents understanding that is gained through knowledge. All the experiences one has with siblings, neighbors, community connections, and education contribute toward this understanding as well as to the general quality of one's mind. The Gemini house represents specific activities within whatever are the boundaries of the community, and these activities contribute to the level of the 3rd house functioning. Thus, Gemini on the 7th house can indicate personal relationships or contacts within the community which contribute to 3rd house knowledge in a particularly important way.

The sign on the 3rd house shows your psychological needs for understanding and your attitudes toward the people and activities of the house, as well as your general attitudes and ways of learning. The ruler shows a personality function most strongly operative in your mental growth in this house and its position shows how you fill the need and what brings out the attitudes. You find how stable you are mentally when you try to combine your own ideas with others' (9th). Can you find greater meaning within broader structures of thought in the outside world without losing your own unique ideas?

Planets in the 3rd house bring a unique emphasis and characterization to your attitudes toward education and knowledge in general. As mentioned earlier, a stellium is not only powerful, it often causes confusion. A stellium here brings mental confusion as one needs to learn to deal with such a variety of totally different concepts and mental associations. Planets in any house always bring people to your life who are related to that function and express the nature of the planet and house it rules. Pluto in the 3rd house has some interesting possibilities, for example. In some cases it shows a drop-out, in others a skipped grade. In both cases, Pluto shows mass influence either from the system which encouraged the acceleration or from the "gang" influence to drop out. In one chart neither of the above happened but the individual was a teacher who felt she was contributing something more than merely what the system officially tries to accomplish. She felt her own educational needs were not met at the personal level and dedicated herself to meeting those personal needs in her students.

13.

Cancer, Moon,
& the 4th House

Cancer represents all past experiences from yesterday to babyhood, and perhaps beyond, which shape your responses and habit patterns. This past experience is the matrix out of which you as an individual must emerge continually as a separate identity (Aries). Before birth the mother provides the initial matrix (amniotic fluid) for growth toward physical emergence. Later, as the mother-image becomes internalized, the people and experiences of the Moon's house provide further nurturing which continually remind you of that earlier experience.

The house of Cancer provides a total surrounding condition for sustaining personal emergence, and is dependent on the Moon's experiences for its effectiveness. In Cancer, you are looking for emotional security either through close, warm human relationships or through substitutes (memories of the past, collections, a business or domestic activities). The imaginative dream-images of the real inner person need to be nurtured in the house of Cancer so they can be expressed in the house of Leo. You may want to be dependent on someone or something here, but if you feel secure within yourself, you may want to "mother" someone or something else.

Cancer is the image-making, form-building sign, since this is where the memory-images are stored. That is, it describes where you are building forms, or images, for the emotions to use—family trees, pictures with sentimental value, a clear image of how you want your house to look, your business to operate—and then working within the image. Or they can be religious symbols, used over and over again, books containing knowledge of the past which makes your cultural heritage more clear and conscious. All these things give you a feeling of emotional security because they form structures within which otherwise unintegrated emotional reactions to Aries, Taurus and Gemini experiences can become focalized and safely experienced. The danger, however, in relying heavily on these external things for emotional satisfaction is that you avoid recognizing your true emotions and finding a deep "center" of security *inside* yourself. Without these safe boundaries, however, insecurity results in over-sensitivity. The emotional reactions become threats to the security, and therefore you build walls around yourself so others cannot arouse the sensitive emotions.

THE MOON is the mother-image, showing the way you responded to your mother, but not necessarily the way she was objectively. (The 4th house ruler comes closer to doing that.) By house position the Moon shows the experiences to which your emotions are most susceptible, due to your past experiences. It is where your mother has most affected your emotional responses, personal habits and your own ability to be a mother—therefore it describes your mother-image. The house and sign position of the Moon defines changes causing emotional reactions which call forth the Cancer images (which can be so devastating without those safe structures). Keeping one's emotional responses flexible in the Moon's house minimizes the emotional stress in Cancer's house, helps sustain emotional stability and leads to emotional fulfillment in Cancer.

The Moon, being the fastest moving body, applies to all the other planets by aspect or phase. This means that all other planets are defining, influencing or shaping the emotions in their attempt to reshape the past. It would be well worth the reader's time to list the Moon's aspects or phase relationship to every other planet to see this in operation. The following may help you do this.

MERCURY/MOON: Your ability to intellectualize or communicate your emotions. Mercury is the defining function as it brings the unconscious memories (Moon) to the conscious level so they can operate rationally.

VENUS/MOON: Your values and ability to cooperate with others (Venus) shape your emotional responses in relationships.

MARS/MOON: Your actions and desires define and stimulate your emotional reactions.

SUN/MOON: Your present consciousness is trying to re-direct your past responses into a new purpose.

JUPITER/MOON: Your principles and philosophies shape your emotional responses and expand the "mother" side of your nature.

SATURN/MOON: Emotional responses and habit patterns are defined and shaped by society and the father, showing how you handle your place in society on a daily basis, or how the unconscious side works with the conscious ego.

URANUS/MOON: Your intuition is trying to universalize your responses to others and make you more aware of their needs. Your unconscious urge for freedom from outdated structures changes your emotional responses.

NEPTUNE/MOON: Neptune dissolves the boundaries of the strictly personal side of your mother image and emotional responses in order to make the mother urge more universal.

PLUTO/MOON: Your unconscious urges stimulate compulsive emotional responses in order to bring emotional regeneration.

THE FOURTH HOUSE is where you build your subconscious self-image and personal emotional foundations, based on early home relationships and experiences which led to successes or failures of the first house image. You have learned to feel a certain way about yourself through experiencing other people's reactions to you, because the sense of belonging is vital to a secure self-image.

The sign on the 4th house shows how you see your mother, and the ruler shows what you saw her doing in your childhood. At the subjective level, the sign on the 4th house characterizes your unconscious self-image, negatively or positively, according to the aspects to the ruler, and its house and sign position. We all identify with our subjective experience of our mother's acceptance of us, which explains many otherwise unexplainable actions. (We have found some situations where the 4th house seemed to represent the father, but more study needs to be done before this can be determined in any individual chart. We suspect that the 4th house always shows the mother, but that sometimes there is a transferral of certain feelings from the mother to the father at some point, which confuses the issue and could be shown in a variety of ways in a chart.)

Planets in the 4th house intensify the need for solid emotional foundations in order to fill the needs of the houses they rule. The following section is a key to the interpretation of the individual signs on the 4th house cusp. Remember that the ruler by house, sign and aspects describes the inner self-image.

Building Foundations:
Signs on the 4th House Cusp

ARIES: Your inner self-image was probably insecure in your early life, and you have to "prove" yourself to yourself in some way. The only real security Aries ever can find for the inner self-image is "a sense of beingness" or a feeling of being in touch with the "ground of being." This is an active, not a passive, state in which by acting on this sense of beingness, the individual experiences it flowing through him.

TAURUS: Your inner self-image depends on the stable results of your efforts to prove yourself mentally or in terms of possessions (Aries on the 2nd or 3rd). How others in your family circle saw these results when you were a child and responded to them determines how you felt about it. Harmony, stability and beauty in home surroundings, and other material qualities may be very important in building your inner self-image.

GEMINI: You can intellectualize about your self-image but you are probably not very deeply in touch with your actual feelings about yourself. Your parents likely fostered a mental approach to emotional matters. Since Mercury rules this part of you, you need to see yourself as a knowledgeable, intelligent person and the degree to which you can achieve this determines the fulfillment of your self-image potential.

CANCER: Home, heritage and family ties can, in themselves, become symbols of your inner self-image. The "mothering" you receive from others, at any period of life, may seem in your eyes to be an indicator of what they think of you, and therefore determine what you think of yourself. This often fosters a negative psychological dependency on family and the past, if the Moon has hard aspects.

LEO: For a strong inner self-image you need to feel you are the center of your home and that it is something you can be proud of. As a child you wanted the activity to revolve around yourself, and the position of the Sun may give some indication of the ease or difficulty with which you accomplished that, and perhaps show the methods you used. Pride in social or family background can be strong here and may become an ego-trip in negative cases.

VIRGO: You need to feel you are perfect, and you may extend this need to your surroundings by keeping the perfect house. In many cases the person with Virgo on the 4th house is so self-critical that he or she can never develop a satisfactory inner self-image. Basically, the early home atmosphere may have been critical and rather cold and the person overcompensates by *using* intellectual superiority as a self-image. The most positive approach to the Virgo self-image seems to be to try to see yourself as a flexible, efficient sort of person who can analyze your surroundings, make adjustments to them, and operate effectively on a personal basis, eliminating superfluous activity and being generally helpful to others.

LIBRA: You need to see yourself as an equal to others in order to gain a firm self-image and foundation. This can be a dilemma in childhood, because obviously you are not going to feel equal to your parents. The Libra fourth house child may struggle in a variety of ways, attempting to find a way to balance the relationship. Some may be combative while others may use more subtle or manipulative ways. The ruler may give some clue as to how it will work in the individual chart since Venus describes one's capacity to relate. Stable emotional foundations and inner self-image come when you can consciously consider the needs and opinions of others to be equally as important as your own.

SCORPIO: In order to find secure emotional foundations, you need to be deeply, emotionally involved with family and home, or something that gives you a sense of belonging. Personal stability and a sense of emotional foundations come with the ability to control your own deep, subconsciously-motivated emotional patterns rather than attempting to control the lives of others. You must be intensely involved in building foundations for the security of others as well as yourself. This may refer to home or larger matters, such as corporations, government, etc. There is a need to transform this area of life and therefore you may experience every level of emotion possible. The inner self-image comes through the deeper relationships you have with others, or the frustrations you have in trying to form them.

SAGITTARIUS: Home may be only a place to hang your hat. The self-image depends on the basic principles and values and the goals that you pursue. You need your personal freedom to move out and enlarge your horizons, making it possible to build your personal foundations or emotional structures. You need to be free to walk out the front door and stay out for a while.

CAPRICORN: You need the security of a respectable home because this signifies to you that you are a respected member of society. You need to feel as though you are a part of the social structure, and your social worth becomes your personal worth. The home and family is where you feel your heaviest sense of responsibility, and this creates an urge to build your inner self-image in a positive way.

AQUARIUS: You build your self-image on your humanitarian ideas, your rebellious activities or just your innate need to be unique. Many children with this position are brought up in group situations, either due to break-up of the home, or the unusual lifestyle of the family. Others go through changes which challenge them to be more independent. Universal attitudes of brotherhood fostered in the home develop your inner self-image.

PISCES: These people will probably never be able to define their feelings about themselves. They have to dissolve old, materialistic self-concepts, and they can't base their self-image on what others think of them. At some time in their lives they may have to walk away from the earlier image, and do it before they have prepared new emotional foundations on which to stand. Basically, Pisces on this house shows that they need to see themselves as spiritual beings rather than material or physically-oriented beings.

14.

Leo, Sun,
& the 5th House

The house on which you find Leo shows the potential fulfillment of ego needs and describes the sense of purpose. In the matters of this house you need to dramatically express your Aries identity, Taurus values, Gemini knowledge and Cancer feelings in everything you do in order to see the reflection of yourself or your inner ideals. Making an impression on your environment is your way of proving to yourself that you are a distinct individual. Leo is the sign of "individualization." Through the activities of this house you can best express the fullness of the developed personality which first emerged as a subjective awareness in Aries. In Leo it becomes full self-consciousness. That is, you were aware of a sense of identity in a very limited or undefined way in Aries, but in Leo you become fully conscious of the nature of that selfhood and its possibilities for power. In Aries you felt the sense of creation or of being created anew. In Leo you feel the power of being the creator.

You need to put your whole heart or emotions into the experiences of the Leo house. Here is where you can most strongly express your generosity, warmth and love in order to promote growth at the personal level. Here you can be an authority, but you should ask yourself whether the reason you want to be one is because you actually have the ability, or because you want to dominate. This is where you have to stand out as an individual, and you may do so, for example, by your clothing (1st), the way you decorate your home (4th), the people you draw into your life (7th), or your professionalism (10th).

Are you putting on an act to get what you want? Or is what you have really 14 carat? There are dangers in the power of Leo (the personality). Because you can create your universe to a certain extent, you may find yourself "playing God"—identifying with the process. In Jungian terms, you have identified your conscious ego with the wholeness of yourself, which is far more than the ego. They call this "inflation of the ego"!

If your Cancer experiences brought insecurity, people may sense your need for self-expression in the experiences of the Leo house, and be concerned for you. For example, with Leo on the 8th, people may be trying to find partners for you to become involved with, thinking perhaps mistakenly that you are somehow unfilled. "You're not having any fun in life," they say, particularly if you have Capricorn rising. People with Leo on the 9th sometimes find others unduly concerned about their religious needs. "Are you saved?" they ask.

THE SUN (your consciousness of individuality) lights up the affairs of the house it occupies. Here you find opportunities to exert willpower, direct your actions and understand your purpose in life. You need to be recognized for your Sun's activities as they represent the ego needs which will find expression and fulfillment through your Leo house. The success you experience in the Sun's house, the legitimate pride you take in its activities, the quality of self-will you express, all determine the fulfillment of the Leo potential. By finding a sense of purpose, you develop self-awareness in the Sun's house and express it through the Leo house.

The Sun is the integrator of the chart (personality). It is through your conscious awareness and control of the other personality functions (Moon, Mercury, etc.) that they can be brought into harmonious and purposeful operation. It is said that the Nodes of the Moon represent the major polarity axis of the chart, calling for integration, but is the Sun's consciousness and willpower which can integrate these polarities. (Detailed information on the Nodes is found elsewhere in the book.)

When we mentioned above the idea of ego inflation, we were, of course, speaking of the Sun, which expresses the activity of Leo. Every person is aware of an "I am-ness" in some way. Saturn represents the separative "I," while the Sun represents the "Am." The danger in any personality is the possibility of identifying with the conditioned, conscious "I" rather than with the wholeness or complete essence of the personality represented by the "AM" personality. Because of the large amount of conditioning we experience in our society, Rudhyar says that for most of us the real essence of individuality (Sun) is buried deep within, and we are operating mainly at the level of conscious ego or Saturn/Moon. The ego then appears as egotism or inflation.

The concept of ego has been described so differently by various writers that it has been confusing to relate it to a chart. We find it easier to describe it in this way: The house of Leo shows where we have ego needs, the Sun shows where we can fill them and where the ego is shaped and developed in order to do so. This is the true ego, which all of us have to develop into a strength or self-confidence that will stand up to the fragmenting experiences of life and integrate the various functions or urges within ourselves which conflict or go in opposite directions. This is the hard-won center of consciousness at the personality level, separated out from the total consciousness by Saturn. It is the weak ego which falls apart under pressure. The necessity at times for a "death" of the ego often means just that self-centeredness must go. When people are egotistical in their Leo or Sun activities, they may actually be functioning from Saturn's perspective at that point. Check aspects of Sun to Saturn in this case. Squares and oppositions either challenge the ego to give up old patterns (waning phase) or to become more individualized (waxing phase), bringing extremes of behavior until the lesson is learned.

Phase and aspect relationships to the Sun indicate how the consciousness is affecting or affected by the other personality urges. Earlier we noted that the slower planets shape or define the expression of the faster. It is obvious then that the Sun consciousness is being shaped by six planets (Mars through Pluto). How can the Sun direct and integrate the activity of these functions? First, it is through the activity of these other functions that we gain consciousness. Phase relationships will suggest how that is working in an individual. Secondly, isn't it true that many of us really are at the mercy of our various urges—our desires, our concepts of what others have told us, our reactions to mass consciousness or public opinion, our religious thinking? It seems to us that following this rule of interpretation to its logical conclusion reveals a basic human problem. We cannot apply our will to integrate our lives and direct our psychic energies as long as *we* let *them* rule our consciousness.

We suggest that the polarity of Uranus is necessary for the solution, astrologically and personally. Uranus represents energies from a trans-personal level of being—some call it soul, or higher mind (intuition), or the High Self. Astrologers often call it the inner, unconditioned individuality or uniqueness, of which the Sun should ultimately be a reflection, a carrier of the true soul energies. This inner individuality manifests sometimes as experiences that awaken you to awareness of potentials you did not know you had. It shakes you out of your pre-conditioned (Saturn) self-concepts and limited viewpoints, bringing a truer understanding of your dominion over your personal universe. We refer you to the section on Aquarius and Uranus for fuller explanation and for material on how the Sun and Uranus operate together in phase.

THE SIGN LEO ON EACH OF THE 12 HOUSES of the horoscope can be interpreted as follows, using the Sun as determinator.

Your ability to pursue the sun-purpose and develop conscious integration of all personality factors determines:

(1) The wholeheartedness with which you reproduce the Sun-purpose through what you project.

(2) The self-confidence you have in your own resources and ability to cope with life, the self-esteem coming from the expression of personality in your possessions, clothing, jewelry, furnishings, financial substance, etc.

(3) The creativity of expression of your ideas and ability to recreate your environment in your own image according to those needs.

(4) The level of your emotional foundations and unconscious self-image. The pride you take in your family tradition and background, often expressed through the dignity, love and artistic quality with which you manage your home life. (In one chart with Pluto in Leo on the 4th the person's parents changed their name prior to her birth in order to avoid the racial connotation of the name. She did not know her real name and background until adulthood.)

(5) The totality with which you can express your emotions freely, dramatically, creatively, stamping your individuality on all 5th house activities.

(6) How well you can put your heart into your daily routine and service to others, filling it with your own qualities of individuality, gaining ego-satisfaction through finding meaning and feeling useful.

(7) The degree of ego-fulfillment gained through feedback from others and the pride you take in your role in shared experiences.

(8) The ease with which you relinquish the selfish layers of your ego and risk the investment of your own vital forces, love, emotions, in deeper relationships. (Relationships, as we mention them throughout this book, can imply roles you play with *any*thing or anyone outside yourself. For example, a person might attempt to destroy over-extended ego in order to achieve union with God or a public, as well

as another person. From another viewpoint, a public servant, such as a police officer, may be risking his life to join forces with the government in a give-and-take situation where his salary is the "take" and his energies are the "give.")

(9) Your ability to express your individuality through your own philosophy, principles, ethics and abstract ideas while, at the same time, understanding what is or is not meaningful to those outside yourself.

(10) The social foundation and recognition you are able to build for yourself. The need to take pride in your public image and express your purpose through it requires self-control and the awareness of contributing to something beyond your own ego-glorification.

(11) The ability to blend self-consciousness with group consciousness, maintaining your own individuality while engaging in social experiences.

(12) Your ability to transcend personal ego and surrender self-centeredness and personal dominion over others and know your part in the greater whole.

THE FIFTH HOUSE shows your needs in love, and the way you express your emotions. Here is where you can channel your 4th house emotions into some form of creativity or personal expression. The more emotional you are, the more you need to channel expression into constructive forms of release, and the more you require the personal freedom to do it. Therefore, if the inner security of an established unconscious self-image (4th house) or personal foundation is inadequate, negative forms may be chosen such as promiscuity, gambling, ego-trips, etc. Normally, expression here will be through romantic involvement, recreation, hobbies, work with children (such as teaching), or artistic pursuits.

The ruler of the 5th shows the personality function most strongly involved in filling and developing your creative needs, and its house indicates an area of life where you go out to express yourself. The sign on the 5th shows the attitudes toward and the quality of your creativity. According to your ability to express Sun consciousness in the house of Leo, you are able to get results from the activities of the 5th house, which are governed by the sign on the cusp. All forms of 5th house creativity are simply extensions of yourself as release of emotion built up in the 4th house.

In a nutshell, the Sun's need for self-expression is fulfilled through the Leo experience, which is applied according to the sign on the 5th house cusp. For example, Leo on the 12th house, Capricorn on the 5th, Sun in Virgo in the 1st house. Leo on the 12th house shows that personal ego expression must be transcended. The Sun can only be fulfilled by rising above its own self-centeredness through service to others in a larger relationship to society. Until this is done, the Leo self-confidence is limited. Therefore, Virgo rising is too shy to be self-projective, perhaps because this person is too wrapped up in details of personal development. In this case, the 12th house Leo seems to be limited by, and limiting to, the Capricorn 5th house. Capricorn on any house limits its activities until structures can be built which draw the respect of others. The enlarged 12th house consciousness will contribute to the 5th house expression at a level that not only brings personal satisfaction, but contributes to society. Each house is contributing to the other like a hand-over-hand process of climbing a spiral ladder.

15.

Virgo, Mercury, & the 6th House

The process of Aries through Leo is one of finding out who you are and being able to express that selfhood through the Leo activity. The strong Leo individuality needs tempering and adjusting so that it can operate effectively, cooperatively and productively with others. In Aries you become aware to a new extent that you *are* a self. In Taurus you learn to appreciate your own personal value. You gain knowledge in Gemini. You nurture it in Cancer and express it in Leo. In Virgo, you need to analyze it and discard the non-essentials in order to put it to practical use.

Virgo symbolizes the completion of personal growth—the inner realization of potential perfection. The ego must now contribute to something outside itself in order to feel useful. Therefore, it must perfect its expression. What did you overdo in Leo? In the house of Virgo you are given the opportunity to make adjustments and find better techniques for personal functioning through analysis and discrimination. This urge drives you to analyze your behavior, health, actions, appearance—everything concerning the signs and houses up to Virgo. The urge is to make these parts of your life conform to a growing awareness of something beyond your individual personality. No self-denial is too great if it leads to this goal.

The purpose is to become a better member of society whether in personal relationships or in larger groups. People born with a social sign rising will have Virgo above the horizon. They are more likely to be aware of this purpose, because the Virgo-ruled activity will be oriented to the outside world. With an individual sign rising, Virgo will be found below the horizon. Perfection will be pursued from a subjective point of view. There may be less conscious awareness of the social implication, although the level of Virgo perfection still is the foundation for relationships.

Because of the need to be useful within society, the Virgo qualities are expressed through personal service, such as nursing, diet, hygiene or, on a more intellectual level, in bookkeeping and other detailed types of work such as literary criticism. At whatever level, Virgo shows by house where you need to serve an apprenticeship, learning the techniques of that activity and applying them in a practical way in your personal life.

In the Virgo experience you become aware of the extremes you may have expressed in the Leo house. Your ability to be useful can be impaired by over-expression. You can become ill through overdoing (in Leo) or through consequent repression in Virgo, because neither is contributing anything meaningful to others. Failure to adjust the Leo behavior in the Virgo house is the greatest cause of psychologically induced illness. The quality of Libra fulfillment depends on the Virgo self-adjustments. The main problem of Virgo is the tendency to allow analysis to turn into criticism. Virgos who are criticizing others only meet themselves in others. They are "projecting" their own imperfections onto outside people and things.

People with strong Virgo emphasis are often intellectual with a great interest in detail. However, they can become so involved with the details that they lose the meaning or purpose for which techniques are being learned, or can't see the total picture within which the details fit. (This indicates the need for the Pisces polarity.) In addition to the intellectual tendency, Virgo has its spiritual or religious side as well. Devotion to a "guru" or the practice of spiritual or religious techniques are another level of Virgo designed to diminish ego-centeredness. The catch is that you can easily either become proud of your own humility or entirely caught up in the details of the technique. *Or,* too rigid a self-denial can literally destroy your own individuality. Many people do not realize that you cannot contribute anything meaningful outside yourself if you lose yourself in doing so.

It is interesting to follow Virgo rising through the houses. Obviously, with interceptions, many people will not have the signs equally distributed through the houses. However, by the time you read through the descriptions you will sense that all the qualities of Virgo are based on the meanings of the other signs on their appropriate houses in relation to the first house. (This is true for any sign rising.)

Subjectively, every sign operates in relationship to the other eleven signs on an equal house basis, with the preceding sign always in the 12th house relationship, the following sign in a 2nd house relationship, etc. You can find out many details about the way a sign functions by setting up a wheel with the particular sign on the Ascendant, followed by the others and interpreting the signs on the houses as attitudes toward activities. This is the basis for Solar Chart interpretation and explains why, when birth time is not known, an accurate reading can be given.

Whether you have Virgo rising with interceptions or even Sun in Virgo, you will find meaning in the following twelve house descriptions. The same technique can be used with any other sign rising. For example, with Libra rising, Scorpio is on the 2nd, and it lets you know that repressed desires concerning finances, personal resources, and the sense of self-worth explain the over-emphasis on beauty and nice possessions or harmonious attitudes of Libra rising. For another example, have you ever stopped to consider that behind every over-confident Leo lie deeply hidden insecurities (Cancer on the 12th)?

Virgo Through the Houses

(1) *(Virgo)* Your basic approach to life is through established techniques. It is important to you to handle details efficiently, and to seek out experiences through which you can develop your capacity for useful service. You are analytical in your basic attitude, and usually self-critical. Looking for perfection makes you aware of every imperfection. The sense of ego-limitation (Leo/12th) forces you to face life with others in mind, and often with shyness. Hence the Virgo orientation toward service.

(2) *(Libra)* Virgo rising learns so much from reading and other mental pursuits that he or she has resources based on other people's ideas—cultural resources. You need the support of others' ideas and cooperative relationships with others to build your own self-worth. You need things of beauty around you, and harmonious conditions in which to earn them, but you also need balance here, in attitudes of generosity or stinginess, as well as with your bank book.

(3) *(Scorpio)* Because of the Virgo ability to analyze and discriminate, you are able to discard unnecessary facts and get to the heart of any matter involving knowledge and communication. Deep, strong desires are hidden behind the reasonable Virgo intellectual attitudes, giving them a fixed, controlled way of thinking and communicating. Even though you have the changeableness of the mutable signs, it does not extend to your ideas. You pursue intellectual matters to the farthest possible end, with great persistence and deep desire, often wanting to control others' ideas as well. It is not unusual to find the overly critical Virgo rising with a few mental hang-ups.

(4) *(Sagittarius)* Your unconscious self-image is based on your principles and beliefs. You feel yourself to be a person whose personality expression is based on a strong sense of fair play, with the ability to speak frankly in standing up

for what you believe. (The nature of your beliefs depends upon the position and aspects of Jupiter.) While you feel yourself to be broadminded and philosophical, your Virgo nature can make you very critical of family members who do not live up to your standards. There is almost an escapism about the way a Virgo can find ways of leaving the home situation temporarily when it proves "imperfect." Your fundamental expansiveness makes any place "home" until its imperfections become evident.

(5) *(Capricorn)* The discretion and discrimination of Virgo rising affects your love relationships by making sure they operate in a socially acceptable manner. Your emotions need to find release through structured and well-planned activities, and therefore the romantic expression may often be sublimated into creative activities if society so decrees.

(6) *(Aquarius)* If you have been overly critical in your search for perfection in others around you, your working conditions will require you to make some adjustments. You are drawn toward work of a humanitarian nature, work in which others' goals, needs and freedoms are equally important to your own. Your work or the routine services you perform, can be an opportunity to get out of the structures or limitations of the Capricorn house and express your own uniqueness in terms of the group need.

(7) *(Pisces)* Your Virgo critical attitudes can be projected on to other people, which is why you need a Pisces 7th house relationship to help you see things in a larger sense. You draw people into your life who have some mystery about them. There is something about them which your Virgo need for analysis simply can't figure out. It may be their imagination, talents, capacity for openness and compassion toward those in need, or it may be simply the Piscean *needs* of the other person. People who are at the mercy of their own imaginations and openness, with mental problems, drug or alcohol addictions, loneliness, are negative types you can draw. The positive Pisces types show you something beyond intellectual knowing. The negative

types give you an opportunity to forget your criticism and lose yourself in service to help them. Zipporah Dobyns has called Virgo rising a professional savior, but warns you against trying to "save" your partner or mate. This side of your nature should be an extension of your Aquarian work, and your mate should represent a positive Piscean who has as much to contribute to the relationship as you have.

(8) *(Aries)* Regeneration of the Virgo identity comes through deep involvements in which you give of yourself. Self-centeredness is the part of the identity which has to be given up, and even being self-critical can become a selfish preoccupation. A deep sexual involvement can release you from the emotional inhibitions of the Capricorn 5th house. A deep psychological involvement can release more spontaneity and true individuality into creative activities and recreation. As personal energies are directed toward joint projects rather than self-fulfilling ends, self-consciousness is lost and the Virgo rising person is free to move forward into the broader activity of the 9th house. You prove yourself through your deep involvements and in facing change courageously and flexibly.

(9) *(Taurus)* Virgo rising needs a practical philosophy or religion. Your principles are tangible and of practical use to your life. Your level of understanding here is based on the kind of facts you have stored away, and you are not easily swayed in your beliefs. Your Virgo intellectual curiosity, however, makes you interested in others' ideas, and you are always looking for something useful to extract from them. Even so, it takes tangible *proof* to change your basic beliefs.

(10) *(Gemini)* The intellectual needs of Virgo rising tend to lead you toward a public image that rests on your knowledge. You need a career through which you can gather much knowledge and information, which can be analyzed and put to practical use in your own personal life. You perfect yourself through it and go out to gain added respect as a result.

(11) *(Cancer)* You find your emotional security through your friends and social involvements. You have the mother image in the group, giving your Virgo practical services in return for the warmth and closeness of human relationships. The Moon will show the ease or difficulty with which you can achieve the emotional satisfactions of the 11th house.

(12) *(Leo)* The ego is fulfilled through the services of the 12th house. Whereas Leo tends to want to shine noticeably, here it is kept in the background, while others who are less fortunate are encouraged and developed in some way. Ultimately, the Leo shines through Virgo's unselfish service. If the Virgo identity does not go through the 8th house change, you will feel inadequate in every way, since you will be too self-centered to recognize and feel compassion for others, which is the way to find the one means of fulfilling your ego-needs.

MERCURY, ruler of Virgo, not only receives, records, classifies and communicates information as ruler of Gemini, but also analyzes that knowledge. Mercury's house shows where and how this mental process is shaped and developed, how you make those associations, and how you approach the techniques of discrimination. Since a full description of Mercury's activity is given under the Gemini section, we refer you to that chapter, and will go on here to the consideration of Mercury retrograde. As you are already aware, Mercury direct implies that you are perceiving, classifying and communicating (Gemini) and *then* analyzing and eliminating information, or at least that you can do this when called upon to do so, as in school situations. However, in the retrograde phase of Mercury's orbit, the Virgo process must be completed *before* communication can take place.

THE MERCURY RETROGRADE mind is, in Rudhyar's words, "working against itself." In more common terms, the experiences of the Mercury house are taken inside and analyzed (the Virgo function) first, adjusting them to the person's personal needs and viewpoints. Only then are they dispensed or communicated in the Gemini house, often giving the appearance of slow mental activity, which is completely erroneous. The Gemini knowledge is simply more personalized or individualized in this case. It is especially vital that parents listen to their Mercury retrograde child carefully and make sure they understand what he is saying and that *he* feels he has communicated satisfactorily what is on his mind. Parents who don't have time to listen are inhibiting an already difficult function. The incomplete communications can be turned inward again only to exteriorize later as complexes.

The inwardness and subjectivity of the retrograde Mercury process often makes the individual unusually sensitive to others' communications. He "takes everything personally," as he has to relate all incoming data to himself in order to make it meaningful. Once things are learned, however, they are never forgotten because they have been related personally to the individual. Rudhyar states that Mercury retrograde is seeking a new level of consciousness, which perhaps explains these effects.

THE MERCURY-SUN RELATIONSHIP helps to clarify the direct and retrograde phases of the Mercury cycle. As stated earlier, Mercury communicates the will and purpose of the Sun to the conscious personality. It is never more than 28° from the Sun and is seen following or preceding the Sun in its annual circle of the Zodiac and the individual chart. During its three retrograde periods, it dips down into the unconscious where it picks up the "message" of the Sun at the time of inferior conjunction. At this point it is between the Earth and Sun at "new phase." Then it has the opportunity to communicate this same purpose to all the planets in turn, either as it transits through the sky or, more symbolically, through your chart.

When natal Mercury is retrograde and near the Sun, you are not likely to be objective about yourself. Information gathered is applied and used at such a personal level that relationships are not seen from other people's points of view. When natal Mercury is direct, whether close to the Sun or not, there is more objectivity, reaching a peak at the time of

superior conjunction (full phase) when Mercury is beyond the
Sun at its farthest distance from Earth.

We are of the opinion that the significance of Mercury
combust (within 3 degrees of the Sun) is most applicable to
its inferior conjunction (Mercury retrograde). At this time, the
conscious rational function is being obscured by the "ego" or
material consciousness. The Sun, as we've already said, is only
the "ego" when the personality has denied contact with the
unconscious and is depending entirely on its conscious learned
abilities. Astronomically, and symbolically, this conjunction
takes place beneath the western horizon and is never seen.
Whether this means that a person with Mercury retrograde
conjunct the Sun is going to have his rational powers eclipsed
by his "ego" (Earth consciousness) may depend on other
factors shown in the chart. Its more general meaning is described under Mercury Retrograde above.

THE SIXTH HOUSE represents a critical phase in personal activity. It unites you with others or separates you from
them. What you do with this area of your life determines your
capacity to relate to others on an equal basis. Better techniques for personal functioning learned in the Virgo house
help you to readjust your personality and be more useful and
effective in your routine activity at the daily level (6th). Ill-
nesses related to the 6th house result from inadequate adjustment and are often psychological in origin. Hypochondriacs
are either so self-critical that they feel inadequate and are
using illness as an excuse for not being productive, *or* they are
escaping from the responsibilities of their daily routine. Aspects from Pisces, the 12th house or its ruler, or Neptune may
show escapism. Virgo or Mercury aspects could point to self-
criticism.

Vocational rehabilitation is often the best therapy for
those who are psychologically or physically disabled. The sign
on the cusp defines the quality of activity where you feel the
most useful, and which leads to personal adjustments. Through
work, service or your daily routine, you begin to feel more
adequate as an individual and therefore more capable of cooperative activity. The ruler of the 6th house shows other

personality functions and activities necessary for fulfilling the 6th house needs. Planets in the 6th house represent personality functions needing this sense of usefulness through productive routine experiences in order to fulfill the needs of the houses they rule.

Being so caught up in the daily routine or in personal self-adjustments and desires for perfection that you cannot see your role in the larger whole of relationships or society is a common negative 6th house quality. If the 12th house is stronger, you could be so involved in social service to humanity that you fail to fill your own psychological needs or to see the needs of the individual the group is trying to help. Balance here is extremely important for mental health.

16.

Libra, Venus, & the 7th House

The Aries identity ultimately can only find fulfillment through interaction with others (Libra). This has often been objectified as Man and Woman, the male-female polarity. We call it the "relative identity." Just as Aries is the first step toward personal identity awareness, Libra is the first step toward social identity, which becomes established in Capricorn and expressed in Aquarius.

In this area of your life you feel a need for connection and harmony (often at any cost) with others, through either competition or cooperation. Your Aries identity needs to become aware of others and their needs, and to learn to function with them in a relationship where you both are equal. Contrary to many ideas, Libra is not always experienced in relationship. This sign emphasized may only imply that you need to *learn* how to relate. Balance is needed so that you neither lose your identity nor dominate another's. Social, cultural and artistic activities lead to the refinement of the individual as a social being, because he is seeing and experiencing the values of other individuals. So we see Libra ruling the arts, legal relationships (which keep things "balanced") and various kinds of social partnerships.

Libra often involves some kind of unconscious personality projection because you are looking for the complement to what you already are—a part of yourself you have not brought out. Frequently it is the male looking for his submerged female complement, or the female looking for her submerged male side. Finding this in someone else who is like that part of yourself gives you an objective view of yourself. This view will be satisfying or not depending on what Libra ideal you are expressing, and on the strength of your individuality (Aries through Virgo). You see the results of your own identity activity here, and sometimes pin the Aries need on to a person or persons in this house so that you have difficulty seeing those people as they really are. This has given the Libran a reputation for being a delightful companion in short-term relationships but shallow, manipulating or fickle in more involved relationships.

In the Libra area of your life, you need to share your ideas with others, and therefore must listen as much as you speak. You are looking for an ideal by which to evaluate your relationships, and your ideals must be large enough to include both your and the other's points of view. You will probably be confronted by two opposite ideas here, and your Libra scales must weigh their value and integrate them.

VENUS, by house position, shows what you are evaluating and attracting to yourself in order to fulfill your Libra relative identity needs. It shows what you draw to yourself in others based on your feelings about yourself and your personal values. These people objectify your own feelings. You are receptive toward them because you can identify something of your own nature in them. In other words, Venus gives a clue to the ideal projected in the Libra house.

Traditionally, in a man's chart Venus shows the ideal he is seeking in a female relationship. If his own values are operating positively he will attract relationships characterized by the positive side of Venus' sign. If his values are unstable or too fixed, he may attract a negative manifestation of his Venus sign, objectifying his own need to harmonize his values and balance them with others' values.

In a woman's chart, Venus shows how she feels about herself—how she identifies with her femininity. This is the traditional description of what Venus represents. However, it is not unusual to see a woman drawing male partners obviously characterized by her Venus sign. Also, while Venus has always represented the receptive side of a man's nature, he was taught to identify with it only in the opposite sex, not in himself. This situation has been changing and represents one place where we feel traditional meanings in astrology are no longer adequate.

IF VENUS IS RETROGRADE, the Libra social experiences are personalized. You can't find expression of your personal values and feelings until you re-evaluate your social relationships. This produces repressed feelings, described by house, sign and aspect. You internalize everything concerning a relationship in order to re-build your own personal values. You reverse the natural Taurus-Libra order and base personal values on social ones. (See Venus retrograde under Taurus.)

VENUS IN THE CHART:

1. If Venus is in a group sign (Libra through Pisces) and below the horizon, you need to build your social values into your personality.

    (Venus in a group sign shows well-developed social values. Aspects would show how these values have been used and point toward a possible need to revise these to better act as a social individual. Harmonious aspects would show wise application of social values in relationships. Here, Venus shows that you tend to base your experience on previously formed values.)

2. Venus in a group sign and above the horizon shows well-developed social values are operating out in social situations.

3. Venus in a personal sign (Aries through Virgo) and below the horizon shows you are developing social values in personal areas of life activity (being useful—6th house,

developing creativity—5th house, etc.) in order to be able to relate on a social level. You can't operate on an equal basis with others unless you feel you, yourself, are valuable (Taurus). Personal values must be built in the Taurus house before you can build social ones in the house of Libra.

(Venus in a personal sign shows that your social values are quite personalized, and you are developing them on the basis of personal experience.)

4. Venus in a personal sign and above the horizon shows that you are developing social values through social experiences.

5. If Venus is in a personal house and Libra is above the horizon, your process of building values is brought into your social life. For example: Libra on the 10th house may indicate you apply them to your profession, or at least bring them out where everyone can see.

6. If Venus is in a group house, and Libra is below the horizon, you bring the values you gain from associations into your personal life.

THE SEVENTH HOUSE designates the area of life pertaining to your image of how you take part in cooperative relationships, how you see yourself in relation to others. It shows the side of you that needs others to draw it out. Here you see how you develop as a person in relationships. Are you cooperative or competitive, aggressive or receptive, frustrated or fulfilled? The sign on the 7th house cusp shows how you operate in relationships and the kind of people you need in your life to complement your own individuality.

7th house relationships imply those that exist within a larger framework (such as society or an organization) for a purpose that is more than just personal, or are legalized in some way. For example: business partners, doctor-patient, writer-public, husband-wife, seeker-God. The ultimate purpose of the 7th house is to bring greater awareness at some level, through having to relate to what is different or outside.

The ultimate awareness is to realize that the purpose that brings you together makes you of equal value.

If the ruler of the 7th house is inharmoniously aspected, its position and aspects show the kinds of people you draw into relationships who objectify your own problems in relating. What you see operating through them is a subconscious facet of your own personality being brought out to be developed or balanced. Aspects from the 7th house ruler to other house cusps may indicate the significance of other areas of life affecting relationships.

Planets in the 7th house show other areas and functions that are brought out through relationships and strongly affect them. They need relationships to open their doors (the houses they rule). They show functions of your personality that you are trying to find in others because you are unable to identify with those sides of yourself. Many planets in the 7th house show that there are many needs you are looking to others to fulfill. One person can never fill all those needs, so you will either have more than one marriage, or you will find a number of different kinds of relationships to be involved with at the same time.

If the 7th house ruler is well-aspected but the planets occupying it are not, then these planets show personality functions that interfere with the free flow of an otherwise good potential for harmonious relationships. If the ruler is not well-aspected but the occupant planets are, they show personality functions which will help improve a basic difficulty in relating.

By developing your social values in the Libra house and maintaining harmony therein, you can improve your personal relationships. Taurus values are also significant in terms of the 7th house. Your relative image (7th house) is how you see yourself in relation to another. If your personal Taurus values have brought a sense of self-worth in your 2nd house, you are consciously aware of having something of worth to contribute to the relationship.

17.

Scorpio, Mars, Pluto, & the 8th House

The activity of the Scorpio house is energized by deep, intense, compressed and subconscious desire-oriented emotion which indicates the potential for power. Here, Mars-desire seeks fulfillment through deep emotional involvements with others or something outside the Mars/Aries identity. This can be a desire for control over others in the Scorpio house, a desire often repressed due to social or parental conditioning. Because the power of repressed emotion is so strong, it is imperative to balance self-control with the desire to control others. This desire for personal power over others has to be transformed into desire for the group goal.

You can be a unifying factor in groups connected with your Scorpio house. You may be a focus or channel for group energies contributing to some common goal, whether it is socially constructive or destructive, whether it contributes to group goals or your own personal ends. This power comes from experiences of the deep past, long hidden in the unconscious. When these memories are activated but not understood, you repress them, gradually building up the pressure all out of proportion to the current or original incident. Eventually something happens to release the pressure. If it is released through compulsions, then you have no control over it, and it is harmful both to yourself and others. In many cases there will be a compulsion to control others based on *fear* of the group. However, often the power is turned inward upon the individual, and in this case, Scorpio hang-ups may show themselves in extremes of self-control or self-denial rather than in compulsions to control others. The problem is the same—to find constructive release for repressed energy.

Much compressed emotional content can be released through creative activities as well as sex. (That's why Scorpio is traditionally seen as the sustainment of Leo, and the 8th house of the 5th.) Psychotherapy has recognized this, and there is a great increase of art-music-dance therapy. (We have noticed that people involved in therapy have emphasis on the 8th house, or Scorpio, or their rulers.)

Scorpio represents at its highest level, the deep, transforming power of unselfish love in which one actually "sacrifices" his own ego-centeredness. The individual may allow it to become regenerated by a full merging of self into a total relationship with a person, a group, or with the soul. This is different from Piscean love, although in time it leads to Pisces. Pisces represents the universal life of the already-changed person who loves all as one. Scorpio, however, involves intense personal experiences that deeply change the person.

PLUTO AND MARS: Mars is the personal drive to get what you want. Sometime in the past this drive ran up against social or parental restrictions, because it went against or beyond social or family standards. The unfulfilled desire-energies were repressed in the Scorpio deep unconscious because they were desires involving other people. These hidden energies can control you in some way, such as in compulsions, complexes, blocks to action or fear. Mars' position may in some way show the kind of desire that has been repressed, although much of Mars' activity in a personality is not hidden. However, it does show the orientation of your desire-nature, which defines the repressed energy in a general sort of way.

Pluto is the unconscious urge to contribute to the evolution of society through the deepest reality of your beingness—
a kind of higher vibration of Mars. This urge wants to transform the suppressed energies into desire for group goals and
release them for use in the Scorpio house. Pluto's position
shows the area of life where these personal energies are trapped, or rather, what kinds of experiences will trigger them.
Changes, upheaval, social or other influences will allow them
to be released, transformed and integrated into your consciousness. These activities represent your role in furthering
human evolution. The sign shows the kind of abilities or skills
previously trapped and now seeking release in a new form . . .
Cancer: the need for nurturing and self-protection; Leo: recognition of the need for individualized self-expression; Virgo:
awareness of ecology and the need for efficiency; Libra:
awareness of the need for equality; Scorpio: the need for
power through unity.

Pluto represents the main growing edge of your personality. Roughly two-thirds of your consciousness is trapped in
your subconscious memories. All through the chart there is
evidence of this in squares and oppositions, and with planets in
fall or detriment. These usually involve some conscious versus
unconscious activity. When material is released, the conscious
life expands in a very real way. (Pluto always exposes the
realities of the house it occupies.)

If you have not allowed Uranus to awaken your awareness
of an existence beyond ego-consciousness, if you have not
allowed Neptune to dissolve old ego-boundaries and nourish
the new, more group-oriented consciousness, then Pluto will
release these unconscious energies destructively, either to
yourself or others. If you have been willing to give up some of
your selfish desire out of respect for others, the Pluto energy
will be released constructively, as group power in the Scorpio
house. Your Pluto shows your potential to become controlled
by your urge to participate in the larger whole of humanity.

The house of Pluto always contains an impersonal element,
because personal energies are hidden. It is where you have to

go beyond personal expression and be an example to others. This kind of situation forces you to find a larger framework for the activities of its house, and often just the experience of reaching out to humanity instead of to one individual can be a releasing factor. You will be challenged to change or transform conditions here in order to feel you are a part of something larger than yourself in the house of Scorpio.

In Scorpio the desire-activity of Mars leads either to self-understanding or to control of others. You can either let your Mars rule Aries alone and go selfishly about your own business, or you can initiate those Aries activities within the boundary of Scorpio respect for others' needs for initiative. Aries is personal activity, whereas Scorpio is shared activity.

Is your Mars energy going to operate with Aries selfishness, or are you going to let your desires be transformed to operate with others? Pluto-Mars aspects and their phase in a chart show how you are able to combine your desire-energies productively with others. If Pluto is aspected to Mars, there is a direct connection between conscious and unconscious desire-energy. It can make your actions compulsive. If Mars is conjunct Pluto you may find a tremendously strong energy block or fear and need to withdraw. Strong aggressive drives are suppressed in order to focus your attention on the need for transformation of personal desire. Such concentrated energy can often be released very destructively through violent temper or actions.

Mars in waxing square to Pluto is ready to clear away the obstacles to release the subconscious content, but the result may be destructive on outer levels. Mars in waning square to Pluto shows personal attitudes are being reoriented toward group desires. If in opposition, Mars desire tends to go to some personal extreme to balance the strong pull toward regeneration and release. Here, you have to find a reason outside yourself for controlling your desires for the good of the group. Mars shows that reason by house position.

If Mars and Pluto are conjunct in Balsamic phase, the personal desires are being transformed by Pluto upheavals or changes. In new phase, Mars is projecting the transformed attitudes through the actions. Mars cuts something out of the personality or life, as shown by house and sign. Pluto destroys it, then builds something else.

If Pluto is conjunct a planet, that part of you is subjected to intense pressure to change. Some important energy connected with the planet is being blocked or used compulsively. The orb of aspect may indicate the year of life in which the problem originates (1 degree = 1 year of life). Easy aspects to Pluto show easier transformation or clearing of repression. Hard aspects may show where more abrupt changes or destructive activity forces the transformation. Aspects from the Sun to Pluto show that you can go through change consciously and with a sense of purpose. Easy aspects show an active desire to cooperate with the growth process. Hard aspects show the conflicts between the self and the group identity which challenge the self to take on the struggle to change.

Mars and Pluto, Retrograde and Direct

MARS DIRECT, PLUTO DIRECT: Through Mars, the individualizing force, you go out to "do your thing"—to assert yourself as a separate individual in order to fulfill your personal desires. This invariably leads you into relationships with others who objectify your own hidden psychological problems (Scorpio) which were caused from the frustration of earlier involvements.

Eventually others show you where regeneration or growth are needed (Pluto), in order to become a more other-conscious identity (the re-born Aries). Mars action activates problems. Pluto reveals and changes them, leading to self-understanding for the re-born Aries identity. You will find the activities of the houses containing these signs working in these two "orders": from Aries to Scorpio and from Scorpio back to Aries.

Pluto reveals the subconscious content of problems and forces you to deal with them, leading from self-understanding and transformation in Scorpio to a new sense of identity that

is aware of its total union or involvement with something outside itself, in Aries. Mars then operates on a new level, living
out the new identity.

MARS RETROGRADE, PLUTO DIRECT: (See Mars R. under
Aries section.) Your Mars may only go out to act in its own
interest after you have understood its action, and therefore
you may appear passive. Or, on the other hand, you may act
outwardly with what seems to be Mars' usual spontaneous
aggressiveness. In this case, you will be unconsciously re-
enacting or reacting to some hidden experience that the Mars
house represents. Because Mars R. goes directly to the realm of
Scorpio, these reactions will create stirrings in the unconscious
which awaken Pluto's urge to release the energies. As unconscious desire-energy surfaces and you can see it in operation,
your own urge to live beyond personal desire transforms the
energies and enables them to be channeled *powerfully* into
group activity. If Mars stays retrograde all your life this will
not be as strong. But if Mars goes direct by progression, the
year it changes direction will bring a major change of action in
the Scorpio house.

MARS DIRECT, PLUTO RETROGRADE: Mars takes its
usual direct course of events leading to personal involvement.
But Pluto's role is reversed. Your growth process has evolved
to a point where you need to build deeper personal foundations before you can go on to larger or deeper group experiences. The unconscious urge (Pluto) for a sociologically significant role in life remains unfulfilled until the unconscious
side of the personality has been transformed, and until you
become inwardly what you want to be outwardly. The influence you have on others in the house of Pluto R. is due to
your own *inner* transformation and change (if you accept
change). In any case others will see you revealed to the very
core of your personality in that area. (With Pluto D., others
will see you revealed through what you are doing more than
what you are or how you are living your personal life.)

PLUTO RETROGRADE, MARS RETROGRADE: With both
planets *direct*, a person goes through experiences in the outer
world which bring about personal transformation which he is

consciously aware of. With both *retrograde*, desires (Mars) are repressed, and much activity goes on inwardly (unconsciously) which creates turmoil you do not understand. It may reveal itself through nightmares of highly symbolic nature, violent compulsions or other less dramatic indirect expression, because Pluto R. cannot directly release the hidden energies to the conscious level.

Mars R. has to control personal desires, often through repression, until they are understood, working backward from Scorpio to Aries. But since Pluto R. cannot consciously control or release energies, the transformation must take place first inside, and even then the full conscious release may never occur, probably because it does not need to.

Since Mars R. is in contact with the subconscious, and Pluto R. is operating more deeply than usual in the psyche, there is contact with occult forces of great intensity and power. Even though you are not aware of your own influence on others, they are learning something from you, because they can observe in your life the hidden occult laws concerning death and rebirth. *You* are learning to "let go" of personal desires. Everything you sacrifice on the conscious level transforms or releases some hidden repressed energy because it was created originally through a similar experience in the past.

Although newly-acquired knowledge of the human psyche has revealed this overall Pluto/Mars process, there is still little that can be said definitely about how the process will operate in an individual chart. Mars/Pluto, direct or retrograde, may or may not show violence, disaster, death and sexual hang-ups. They may or may not show a kind of genius based on contact with the mysterious complexities of the subconscious mind.

Mars activity alone, because of its conscious and long-observed action, is fairly simple to define in an individual chart. But its connection with Pluto is not. After all, the drive toward individualization of the personality created the subconscious in the first place. The Lord of the Underworld holds no keys to the purpose and directions of the God of War, and they who would understand the meaning of the human spiritual journey must first take the path into their own darkness to meet death and rebirth. Perhaps only then can they understand another's path and interpret it in a chart.

THE EIGHTH HOUSE is called the house of separation, death, re-birth, sex, sacrifice, ritual, taxes, etc. It shows the results of 7th house relationships. The level at which you approach the Scorpio house, which is largely determined by Pluto and Mars, helps or hinders your effectiveness in getting results out of relationships. The regenerated attitude of the sign on the 8th house makes it possible for you to become more productive in your joint efforts, which in turn, releases you from personal limitations. Personal limitation in the 8th house sense concerns your productivity, which is limited when you operate alone. It is multiplied when you unite your own resources and abilities with those of others.

In psychological terms, the sacrifice experienced in the 8th house refers to the sacrifice of the ego, time, material resources and personal desires as a joint contribution to multiply your individual potential. Some psychologists believe that planets in the 8th house represent psychological functions which are denied or "sacrificed" at some period in life. Some personal facet of the function has to be changed in order to work jointly. This means it has to be raised to a more than personal level.

For example: The Moon in the 8th often means the mother image does not reach completion. Either the mother is not close either physically or in other ways. Or, you feel rejected (often unconsciously), or you felt your mother was inadequate, which stimulated you to take over the mother's role prematurely, which means that for part of your life you play the mother role in an "adolescent" fashion.

The Sun in the 8th house often shows one who is late to mature. A deep intense sense of purpose drives you to maturity but a super-strong ego has to be transformed first. In maturity you should be able to direct your energies in such a way that others are included and not hindered. In extreme cases, you appear almost childishly wrapped up in your own concerns. In any case, your intense energy drive puts you in close contact with others so that your ego is being continually sensitized through involvements with them.

The 8th house call for sacrifice also shows why big business and taxes come under its jurisdiction. Big business is a combining of people's efforts toward the goal of corporate profits. Taxes are a combining of people's money toward the joint goal of building roads, supporting government bureaucracies, etc. An inheritance is money that comes from other people. Death is the overcoming of physical limitation by sacrificing the body in order to join with something greater. Therefore, this is also the house of the astral body and reincarnation. The 8th house also rules rituals through which you call upon the forces of the unseen to augment your personal power. Thus, it rules the occult. The sign on the 8th house shows an attitude or quality that needs augmenting or to be regenerated if you are to obtain the results you are looking for in a relationship. The ruler shows through what experiences you will find it.

18.

Sagittarius, Jupiter, & the 9th House

Sagittarius is the last of the fire signs and the first of the universal signs, holding the key to the transcending of the personal will and purpose of the Sun. The aspirations and religious or philosophical beliefs acquired here allow you to set your goals for future success in Capricorn. Here you are able to gain wisdom from mutual sharing of ideas, which leads to a larger point of view and a broader understanding of life through the relationships you encounter. You begin acting on the basis of abstract principles, ideals, beliefs and values.

What you do in the house of Sagittarius provides self-improvement in the house of Leo. Every house provides a structure with a boundary (cusp), which is a Saturn principle. In the house of Sagittarius you may feel hemmed in, creating the urge to run away, to escape from the boundaries of reality of that activity. These boundaries may create frustration, but are necessary until the Capricorn foundations are adequately developed to support your expansive ideals.

In Sagittarius, you want to move out into the larger group, expressing what you have found to be meaningful in your own life. This is why Sagittarius is the teacher's sign. But who learns more than the teacher? You gain new ideas and broaden your own philosophy until you realize your Capricorn structures are no longer adequate.

Something died in Scorpio in order that a new goal, a new vision could be seen in the house of Sagittarius. However, if the self-centered desire of Mars did not die in the Scorpio experience, Sagittarius will expand his sphere of influence for personal gain, regardless of the needs of others. Or, his natural honesty of expression can be simply a bluntness that can hurt others, resulting from lack of sensitivity.

Your degree of honesty may be determined by how you dealt with the previous eight signs. If personal values were not built in the house of Taurus, you may have no consideration or understanding for the difference between what is yours and what is not. Without the necessary facts (Gemini) to back up your more abstract concepts you may turn to over-exaggeration, even deceit. Aspects from Jupiter or planets in Sagittarius to planets in the first eight signs will indicate the use of the Sagittarian energies of expansion. Squares to planets in these signs suggest an incomplete development of attitudes toward the affairs of the houses.

You released power in the Scorpio house. How are you going to direct it? That is the problem of Sagittarius. Sagittarius is the goal seeker. With the energy of the horse beneath you and the intellectual understanding of your human potential on top, you have the strength and wisdom to move out into the broader realms of social experience with confidence and faith. This is represented by the symbol of Sagittarius, the human torso on the body of a horse. This strength and knowledge enables you to consciously shoot for your goals (represented by the arrow of the archer). Which half will outweigh the other—the animal or the intellectual? Is the need for freedom expressed through expansive ideals or expansive living?

JUPITER'S position in the chart shows the activities through which your basic social principles and ethics are shaped and developed. In early life this will include schooling, religious education and family background for everyone, but the house of Jupiter will show a specifically important area.

Jupiter goes out to more expansive experiences in order to bring broader horizons to the Sagittarius house. Ordinarily speaking, Jupiter allows you to expand some area of your life in compensation for the limiting function of Saturn in its house. With the underdeveloped Saturn, Jupiter may expand excessively in some area—such as over-eating, over-spending, fanatical religious attitudes, or over-learning without assimilation of facts. Jupiter rules the process of assimilation on physical, mental, emotional or spiritual levels. As the liver produces bile to digest food, your religious, moral, ethical and social background produce personal principles and philosophical attitudes that give meaning to factual experience.

THE JUPITER/SATURN function is a compensation activity. Jupiter expands, Saturn contracts. What does this mean to you? We are always trying to expand in some way, consciously or unconsciously, physically, mentally or otherwise. The house of Jupiter shows an area of experience where we *can* expand—up to certain limits. Those limits will be shown by Saturn's position. Saturn's limitations are simply requirements that we learn something, strengthen our position, or take care of present responsibilities before we can go on expanding some more. Expansion requires a solid foundation. This is a good example of the truth that your chart does not rule you—you rule the chart. It is quite possible for you to expand excessively in the Jupiter house, while operating on weak foundations in the Saturn house, only to have the Jupiter affairs finally collapse on you. A Saturn/Jupiter opposition might especially enhance this tendency.

With a conjunction, the expansion urge identifies with the contraction urge. Saturn could crystallize the Jupiter philosophies into a moralistic structure. Or, a constant urge to expand might be continually accompanied by a sense of guilt. Or, responsibilities represented by Saturn could limit the expansion of the house the conjunction occurs in. In perfect balance, such a conjunction shows a strong sense of social and spiritual responsibility with the ability to expand through its projection.

The phase relationship shows the natural way of handling these two opposite urges. The Part of Expression of Saturn/Jupiter shows the area of life where your social responsibilities most actively operate. The last conjunction of Saturn/Jupiter (by house and sign placement in your birth chart) before your birth, is said to indicate "your niche" in life. Escobar says, in "Sidelights of Astrology," "It serves to indicate the native's real niche in life, his sense of belongingness and of being accepted or of being rejected, his sense of adequacy or of inadequacies. I believe it shows the pattern of his generation and how and where he might function best in that pattern with a sense of soul satisfaction."

JUPITER RETROGRADE: If Jupiter is retrograde, the social function is inhibited in some way. This is not intended to imply that you are unable to operate in social situations. It does, however, indicate that there is some problem in attitudes connected with social participation in the activities of the house involved. The dispositor should show the source of the problem. When retrograde, Jupiter has to learn the Pisces lesson of faith and commitment before being able to successfully expand mentally and make larger contacts or apply personal principles in the activities of the Sagittarius house.

The experiences of the Jupiter retrograde house may present you with some frustration concerning your ability to expand socially. For example, if Jupiter is retrograde in the first house, you may be your own worst enemy. What you project may limit or work against your own desire to expand. You may over-eat, creating an unpleasant appearance. You may take in too many unnecessary facts without putting them into useful, meaningful or practical usage. The function of retrograde planets is to reshape their urges. It is not unusual to see the religious structures or philosophy which were ingrained by early conditioning needing to be rebuilt or made more personal to meet the individual's needs.

THE NINTH HOUSE: The ninth house represents all experiences which expand your mind and help you form your philosophy or ethical and religious understanding of life. Therefore this house rules religion, higher education, travel (which broadens your knowledge of culture) and law (which establishes the rules for collective conduct). The wider knowledge you gain here enables you to adjust personal attitudes and ideas to collective concepts.

The sign on the ninth house shows the nature of your philosophy and ethical basis in life and what your needs in formulating them are. The ruler shows where you go out to gain the experiences which shape and develop your philosophies. Your tenth house reputation will be based on the quality of these principles and thus, your ability to operate on a social level. If you did not unite your energies with those of another or others in the eighth house, you will not be able to expand meaningfully within society because you are still operating on an individualistic level. You will not be able to incorporate what you learn from others into your own way of life. You will be like the wanderer who aimlessly travels through life, gathering experiences for no purpose other than personal interest.

The ninth house is where you contact *man's* concept of God through the church or other structures of *revealed* wisdom. If these concepts meet a response within you, they will send you forth on your own personal search for God in the tenth house, where you will want to contribute to the larger whole. The ninth house sometimes operates at multiple levels. If you are searching for a public image (10th), then according to society's rules you need the education to back you up. If you are searching for a way to contribute to society, then this is based on your beliefs, etc. If you are searching for God, you need a religious or occult experience that initiates you into the wider mental awareness of a divine source of life. You can become one with this source in the twelfth house which contains those experiences (such as meditation) which help you overcome "karmic" limitations.

19.

Capricorn, Saturn, & the 10th House

Capricorn is probably the least understood sign of the zodiac. Occultists say it is the most spiritual, and we are therefore not ready to understand its meaning until we become more evolved. According to Alice A. Bailey, even the symbol for this sign has never been drawn accurately. We feel that a psychological understanding of astrology helps us to find new and greater meanings in the 10th sign, and perhaps this is a step toward understanding its more ultimate meanings.

The Capricorn house shows where you need a solid sense of social identity. Saturn shows how and where you build the necessary inner structures of practical relationships to the world that develop the social identity of Capricorn. The 10th house is the actual objective image you have in the world's eyes. Saturn will show how and where you build the outer structures needed for society to accept and recognize you.

In the Leo house you became as fully individualized a person as you are able to be in this life, a person aware of your own selfhood. Capricorn represents the *goal* of individual selfhood—to be a responsible member of society, an individual with your place among all other individuals. You still fully maintain your own separateness, but also carry responsibility for some segment of collective substance—money-power, land-power, people-power, food-power, mind-power, etc. It is the natural need for separateness that often gives Saturn and Capricorn such a negative connotation. Most people need much experience in coping with the extremes of the Saturn side of themselves. They may see their separateness as a verti-cal pattern in which they are "greater" than others, or they remain chained to their deep sense of inadequacy or guilt. Sometimes they do both in two different ways.

As long as you express one of these attitudes, you have identified with the idea of separateness rather than equality. If you have gained the respect desired by the Capricorn house through dominating (at the risk of hurting other people), or out of duty rather than conviction, or as compensation for guilt feelings, then the boundaries you have built between yourself and society have become crystallized. You have separated yourself so completely that you can no longer re-late as an *equal* with others. The results of this crystallization will be seen in the Capricorn house, but Saturn's position and aspects will show the cause. In the Capricorn house you have to live within the laws, principles and limitations of society and also with those attitudes and patterns within your own psyche that are the result of social/parental conditioning. Until you find a productive way to do this, there will be no struc-ture through which the trans-Saturnian planets can operate in your conscious life. (They will still operate, but as unconscious urges only.)

At first, you may feel inadequate in your Capricorn house, because you are still building your own boundaries and pat-terns of functioning there. Also, Uranus will show where you rebel against the pressure of the structure, or where you can bring something new into it. Too much rebellion too early may make it difficult to build a satisfactory practical relation-ship to society.

The psychological meaning of Capricorn and Saturn is to establish a useful, functioning position within society, fulfill-ing your responsibilities to others without demanding from, or relying upon, the rest of society for the ego-satisfaction of recognition of your own superiority. True authority and acknowledgement is *given* to the individual by society in recognition for his actual accomplishments, no more or less. (Saturn rules Karma, the law of cause and effect, whether you see it in terms of one life or of many.) If you separate yourself by building ego-walls around yourself, society will do the same thing to you. It won't let *you* in when you knock at the door.

Capricorn is where all the characteristics of the society-formed ego operate. Because of the social implication, you are looking for respect from others, but you have to be responsible and ambitious to gain that respect. Depending on your ego-strength (the combination of Sun and Saturn), you persevere in the face of any obstacles. President Nixon (Sun in Capricorn) said, in the face of public disapproval, "I won't give up." He indicated it was his *father's* influence that taught him to stick with a rough situation to the bitter end. And it is the father in general who determines consciously and unconsciously the basic attitude toward one's place in society. Planets in Capricorn will have their functions conditioned in some way by the father. The activities of the house of Capricorn operate under attitudes conditioned by the father, knowingly or not.

SATURN represents the way you responded to your father's discipline, authority and example. It *may* present an objective picture of the early relationship, but often it does not. It only can be said to show in all cases how you responded as an individual to him. Aspects to Saturn show more than anything else where you felt conflicts or ease of relating with the father, and the phase-aspect key elsewhere in this book can usually describe quite graphically the quality of response. Aspects to faster planets will indicate the purpose behind the particular father you had, since the faster planets show some past condition or attitude out of which the father-relationship forces you to struggle. Aspects to outer planets show subconscious urges or social influences trying to transform the father-image resulting from the relationship.

In later years, probably beginning at age seven, but reaching a possible conclusion at age 28, Saturn influences become internalized and are called "the father image" or "father figure." Saturn then comes to mean your response to all authority and social structure and your own sense of "inner authority." In other words, if your father taught you never to tell a lie, and you only refuse to tell them because you are afraid of your father's discipline or of the law's discipline, your father image is not internalized. When you choose to tell the truth because you, yourself, believe this is the right thing to do, the image is internalized. It becomes your own inner authority. If you tell the truth, however, because you are afraid of feeling guilty, you are afraid of your own, now-internalized father image.

Because the father is usually the first person you see going out into the as-yet-unknown world and returning at night with announcements about how he relates to that world, it is the father who conditions your own future relationship to society. Even the fact that you may say, "I'll never be like my father" is a result of his influence on your life.

What about the person who has had no father, or one who is seldom around? He may be finding father images around him, but in any case the absence, too, is a father-influence of a reverse nature. Saturn will indicate how you respond to this kind of influence. You often find Saturn retrograde in the charts of people with little or no father relationship, or who have rebelled against the father's influence. Sometimes you find Saturn in the 8th house suggesting a father who spent much time away from home earning money for its support, or in the 12th house sometimes showing a father who was physically, emotionally or mentally ill. With Saturn in the 7th you probably do not identify with the father-image perhaps because he was "distant" in his attitude toward you. In that case, you will be looking for older men or women as mates and partners to fulfill the sense of lack.

Saturn appears in a chart, not to lay a heavy trip on you, but to help you wherever you need the father function of discipline and character to build stronger boundaries of individuality or patterns of behavior. Saturn, the father, is there to help build these patterns, which ultimately fulfill the needs of the Capricorn house. The apparent limitations Saturn imposes are for the purpose of focussing your attention on the true significance of the experience of its house. Until you have understood the deeper significance of the Saturn experience and struggled to find a pattern of behavior, action or thought that fits the requirements of society, you cannot gain the respect needed in the Capricorn house.

Saturn is the structuring, boundary-building function that makes you an individual in your own right, in other people's eyes as well as your own. What goes on in the Saturn house has a crystallizing effect on the developing Sun-consciousness, which is necessary up to a point. (See section on Leo-Sun.) Saturn has a dual function of building both inner and outer structures. Here we would suggest using the word "patterns" instead, such as patterns of behavior, habit, adaptation, learning, relating, etc. The first three refer to the Moon, the other two to Mercury and Venus, all of which are activities that have to be "structured" into patterns acceptable to society to some degree. If the patterns are negative, something went wrong with the father-function.

SATURN/JUPITER/URANUS together are of special importance at this time in our history. Jupiter is the ethical function that represents the principles on which you are building the Saturn patterns. Jupiter is also the social function— going out to be cooperative with others to increase your own gain and expand your own ideas. The way you expand in this cooperative venture is determined by your social values and philosophy. You will note that according to the phase-aspect system Saturn defines or limits Jupiter. This is saying that if your principles are not appropriate to your "station" in life, society will cut you down a notch. You cannot expand socially beyond your reactions to, or attitudes toward, the restrictions defined by your current social environment without repercussions. This limitation does not have to be negative.

Uranus represents that which awakens you to a greater law of existence. If you were born in the slums, your life up to a certain point may be limited by your own "ego-concepts," which were conditioned by the environment. The initial energy of rebellion (Uranus) against conditions may lead to a sudden awareness that you can do more than what society seemed to be telling you is possible.

Saturn is there to focus your attention on the need to build certain structures. When you have consciously seen this need and begun to actually build the new patterns, Uranus may, through some sudden experience, open the way toward the realization that you are more than everyone thought you were, including yourself. With your ego-boundaries enlarged, your ability to expand (Jupiter) finds new fields to explore and greater "wealth" (spiritual or material) to gain from co-operative ventures. It is necessary, though, that the ethical side of Jupiter holds up through the experience. (We refer you to the section on "parts" for further information on the relationship of Jupiter and Saturn.)

SATURN RETROGRADE emphasizes the traditional rulership of Saturn over Aquarius as well as Capricorn. This dual rulership explains Saturn's close relationship to Uranus and also implies that the goal of Capricorn is really equality (Uranus) between separate (Saturn) individuals. Saturn's rulership of Aquarius also explains what happens if Saturn is retrograde. Under this condition, you are unable to build conscious boundaries of separateness around yourself, because in the past you may have had patterns that led to the vertical sense of separateness previously mentioned. You do, however, have subconscious boundaries (often in the form of resentments) that often project negatively and unconsciously. These attitudes need to be reorganized, restructured or repatterned, according to the sign Saturn occupies. For example, in Sagittarius your basic philosophy needs to be not only built on an individual level, but also turned inward to completely re-pattern the subconscious urge to be a separate individual. Basic principles have to become a part of the total being, not just the outer surface.

The inner strength that allows you to stand up for yourself has to be built up from scratch, because there are latent insecurities concerning your adequacy as an individual. These need to be brought to the conscious level and "defined" or re-patterned to develop a more equalitarian (less vertical) way of relating to society. Therefore, as explained in the section on retrograde planets, the Aquarius side of the Saturn function has to take place before the structures of the Saturn house can become effective and your Capricorn identity firmly established in the eyes of others. Service and equality have to become a part of your inner nature before authority can come.

The Aquarius house will show where a new awareness of equalitarian social relationships can be found which will bring out the need and possibility of rebuilding the Saturn patterns. Your ability to reorganize these attitudes will ultimately improve your public identity in Capricorn.

THE TENTH HOUSE shows your basic orientation toward society, and its ruler shows what you need in order to make your role in society real. This orientation comes usually from the father's objective example, although occasionally it is from the mother. Therefore, the 10th house or its ruler will give an understanding of conditions underlying your ability or lack of ability to establish yourself in the outside world.

Everyone needs a social image—a conscious knowing that you belong someplace in the world and are respected for that position. The 10th house ruler shows how you actually gain that image. The sign shows the natural way you can and should come across in public if you are not limited in some way by conditioning. The ruler's aspects show the kind of conditioning you might have sustained. The sign on the 10th house shows a role you play in establishing your personal image on a social level. It also shows the way you have to modify your Ascendant projection in order to make it more acceptable to the outside world. But more than this, the 10th house experience will reveal to you your actual capacity to contribute to the outside world. At some point you have to decide whether to use your public power for solely personal gain or for the good of the whole.

The ruler shows what experiences are needed in order to establish yourself. Therefore, its position will give a clue as to the nature of your ideal profession as well as the ease with which you can gain status through it. Planets in the 10th house show other areas of life (the houses ruled by occupant planets) which depend on your social role for fulfillment of their needs. For example, with Jupiter in the 10th, ruling the 5th house, the urge to expand your social influence through creative expression can only be fulfilled through establishing a social image or reputation. If you are a writer, your books would ultimately sell because of your name.

20.

Aquarius, Uranus, & the 11th House

Aquarius shows where you need to break out of the structures of the Capricorn house when they lose their usefulness, or perhaps to bring new ideas into them. The experiences of the house of Uranus awaken your awareness of this need and open your mind to more progressive ideas. The 11th house represents the social experiences that make you realize the need to be progressive in order to maintain your social image as well as to gain group awareness.

If you become crystallized within the structures you built in the Capricorn house, the respect of others becomes a hollow and meaningless shell which Uranus must eventually crack open if the knowledge and ideals of the Aquarius house are to revive it. The house of Aquarius shows where you may experience unusual conditions and where you can break away from past structured conditions as your attitudes are directed toward the new, the unusual, the modern and the futuristic.

If you have achieved a sense of public identity (Capricorn), Aquarius will represent the ideals under which you can secure that identity through service to humanity. The respect that you gain through the Capricorn experiences becomes meaningful to the group through the service you give in the Aquarius house. The implication of the symbol of the Man with the water pitcher is that the activity of the Aquarius house needs to represent a service performed as an equal which brings a new attitude or sense of freedom to others as well as to yourself. The "special awareness" in the Aquarius house is the capacity to sense what people need, as a whole, but the problem is often in not recognizing the needs of individuals.

While Scorpio has group power in the sense of being able to focus the energy of others toward some kind of goal, Aquarius represents a more conscious form of group power. The Aquarian type can be aware of each individual's function in a group as well as the needs of the group as a whole. He is able to verbalize these needs to keep the group alive through bringing new ideas to its functioning.

Aquarius is concerned with the freedom of individuals within society—at least at the theoretical level. Because of this social idealism, Aquarius frequently finds Capricorn structures too restrictive and either works toward renewing them from within or toward destroying them completely in preparation for new ones. If there is not a goal already conceived, Aquarius can represent pure destructiveness not only on the social level, but on personal levels when the individual rebels against authority without a responsible plan for future constructive behavior. But, however you look at it, there is something unique, cosmopolitan, experimental or "far out" about the house with Aquarius on the cusp.

URANUS, the first of the transpersonal planets, brings sudden changes, separations or other unexpected and sometimes unusual experiences into the house it occupies. Many astrological texts indicate that the transits of Uranus will indicate separation between yourself and the people represented by the house being transited. Perhaps you were dependent upon these people, and the loss creates the sudden realization that you have to look within for your own answers. You discover that you must be centered in your own individuality, as well as have an awareness of being a part of humanity on an equal basis. These experiences open your conscious

mind to the unconscious potentials which go beyond conditioned and trained abilities. Situations are such that you *have*
to call on greater capacities than you knew you had. In other
cases you will feel restricted in the house of Uranus, because
Uranus creates the urge to "break out." You rebel or break
out by bringing the affairs of the Aquarius house into the
Uranus house.

Operating as an unconscious urge for you to be a creative
individual, Uranus also brings inner experiences, such as
flashes of intuitive awareness and images that have power to
motivate the use of your ingenuity. For example, most 14 and
15 year olds (the time of Uranus sextile its natal position) have
a "picture" or "image" in their minds concerning their future
role in life and the ability to do something unique. This dream
is often submerged by material demands and necessities at the
square of Uranus to Uranus around age 21. At 28-30 when
Uranus trines its own position, they must decide if they are
going to materialize their dream into some practical and usable
form, or ignore their own inner creative urge. At 42 (the
opposition), their unique creative potential finds fulfillment
in the outer world if they have made it valuable to others.
Instability also results because they need to change the way
they were previously expressing their Uranian individuality,
or else because they don't accept the deeper significance of
their own individuality with its relationship to that of others.
Thus, at various stages of life, Uranus is concerned with
"imaging" ability, which helps us to discover our creative
potentials.

THE SUN/URANUS POLARITY represents perhaps the
most significant polarity in the chart, but one of which few
are aware. It is the relationship between your conscious personality or "ego" and your unconscious urge to become universalized or more than a separate individual. The phase relationship of the Sun and Uranus will show the uniqueness of
this relationship, further defined by the two parts.

*THE PARTS:**

THE PART OF INDIVIDUALITY is the "Part of Expression" of Sun-Uranus. It shows where you are consciously seeking to express your inner individuality. It is the sensitive point in your chart which characterizes the phase relationship between Sun and Uranus, showing your unique way of expressing the meaning of the relationship in your own life. It is the way you expand your consciousness from a personal to a more universal level, and the area of life in which the expansion is carried on.

THE PART OF IMAGING is where the inner individuality makes use of your conscious purpose and personality energies by "sending you images" or ideas from the unconscious. We feel that the experiences of the house itself are in a sense drawing these images out.

THE PHASES OF THE SUN AND URANUS:

NEW PHASE — The unconscious is spontaneously projecting ideas through the personality. These ideas are often greater than what you could have invented yourself. You may not realize what you are going to say before you say it. Teachers with this phase relationship often learn as much as their students. This phase of Sun/Uranus has a Leo quality because the conscious ego needs to see the unconscious images of Uranus *reflected* (such as by seeing another's response to them) in order to be aware of the reality of the unconscious.

The *Part* shows the area of life and way in which you most naturally project the polarity.

CRESCENT PHASE — Unexpected conditions in the house of Uranus arouse images from the unconscious which bring to the Sun-ego a conscious realization of the need to raise the level of response to the Sun-sign. Conditions from the past in the house of the Sun tend to hold you back, because

---

*See chapter 6 for the calculations of these parts.

your security is being challenged. You may have depended on a more material side of the Sun-sign. Your inner individuality is trying to show you how things should be by sending images and ideas from the unconscious. Or, there may be sudden upsets in the Uranus house that show you the need to depend no longer on the past.

The *Part* shows where and how the energy generated by the struggle is most naturally expressed. That house is strongly affected by the strength with which you struggle out of the past.

FIRST QUARTER PHASE — This is *not* a struggle to become conscious of attitudes and conditions that prevent you from expressing something new and more universal. You already *know* you want to do that. But there are still old conditions that stand in your way. You may meet or create a crisis as you move out to express the new and are confronted by these old conditions (in the Sun's house). These will probably be actual outer conditions, but they will also represent a battle with your own ego. Will your methods be destructive to others, which would show ego-desires at work, or will they only destroy what is truly no longer useful, so that you can build new structures?

The *Part* shows where you are actively and aggressively clearing away old structures related to the house of the Sun in order to find an outlet for the conscious expression of the Uranus images. This outlet will be found in the house of the Part. Its manner of operating is described by the sign.

GIBBOUS PHASE — Early in the Gibbous phase, conditions in the Uranus house are stimulating you to express the new and original in such a self-confident manner that it is highly irritating to others because you have not learned a good technique for expressing individuality. Around 150° the personality is becoming aware of the need to learn better techniques and to perfect the channels of its own uniqueness. Between 150° and 180° there is an increasing urge to let your originality be of some value to others, because you realize there is greater significance or meaning in it than you can understand. You are searching for this meaning.

The whole point is to analyze the way you are being an individual and come to realize that your true individuality is a universal value (Uranus) rather than a separate one (Saturn). This phase is Saturn-ruled, indicating conflict between the ego-conditioning that tells you to be separate from others and the inner being which wants you to become a part of the whole. At the same time, the Saturn quality is necessary as it builds the structures which Uranus needs to fill (at full phase). Therefore, you cannot choose one over the other. You need both, and at this phase you are searching for a conscious understanding of how you can bring them together.

The *Part* shows the most characteristic or natural way in which you go about analyzing and perfecting the polarity as shown by the sign. The house shows the activity through which it can most easily be expressed.

FULL PHASE — This phase usually shows a considerable measure of maturity and consciousness in using the forces of one's own genius, after resolving the initial instability or ambivalence regarding tension between the ego and inner self. You are confronting opposing forces in yourself which are objectified in your outer relationships. Through dealing with them you become aware of something you never knew you had. Separations and differing viewpoints may be part of the circumstances, but through them can come revelations of a most unusual nature. They may simply be weird ideas with no substance, if you are unable to find a deeper meaning. You may believe that you have just had a fantastic vision and must rush out to communicate it to everyone. You *do* need to express these ideas and experiences, but it is important that you remain open to others' experience at the same time.

The *Part* shows where and how the instability or the realizations are going to find their most natural outlet.

THE DISSEMINATING PHASE — The inner self is established in the consciousness and fills you with an urge to go out and express something with inner meaning to others. This can take the form of inciting others to rebellion (especially if sesquisquare) or of sharing new ideals of freedom. These ideals have to be meaningful to you. If not, then you are sharing something empty which simply arouses others to an irrational need to break out. At its best level, Uranus is flashing you images that make you aware of higher values and meanings in larger relationships. Your ideals are universal in quality. The contacts you make arouse further images from the inner self as one's Sun approaches the end of the phase, and these realizations open up new areas of investigation, making you aware that there are still further reaches of true individuality.

The *Part* shows the area of life and the way in which you go about sharing your most universal ideals of freedom and group relatedness.

LAST QUARTER PHASE — Something happens to bring disillusion with the ideals with which you have been brought up. You need to reorient your conscious ego to new, more appropriate ideals. The originality behind your conscious direction and purpose at this point often is represented by people outside yourself from whom you are learning a need for different, higher principles of relating to society. The awareness grows within, while outwardly you wear the mask of your old ideas. The closer you are to the square aspect, the more suddenly and forcefully the mask will drop, and the new individuality emerge. If you did not build a new set of ideals after the disillusionment, your response to this phase may be pointless rebellion or perhaps illness.

The *Part* shows the area of life most strongly affected by the reorientation of your purpose by your inner individuality and where you have the best chance of expressing the newly created individuality.

BALSAMIC PHASE — Your inner self is sending you images that compel you to re-evaluate your conscious direction and purpose in the house of the Sun. Prophetic glimpses of the future make you want to commit yourself to a new, higher level of group-consciousness. You sense a need to eliminate old personality patterns in order to be a channel for the new. You feel isolated either because you feel inferior to the new vision or because you are living out something others don't understand. In any case, you sacrifice something of your personal consciousness in order to become more universal.

The *Part* shows the outlet for this sense of dedication, and will be in the late 11th or 12th house, possibly even the 10th, indicating that new ideals of social service are part of the vision.

THE ELEVENTH HOUSE: The meanings of the 11th house have expanded in recent years as man's awareness of his involvement with society has expanded. It is, however, in the 12th house that we find true oneness with, or at least dedication to, the wholeness of life. In earlier years, when human consciousness was insular, 10th house goals for achievement were more personal, and the 11th house was legitimately a house of personal hopes and wishes and friendship. In more recent times, with the birth of labor unions and, at other levels, local groups of all kinds, people are finding more opportunity to reach goals unattainable without collective action.

The 11th house represents the results of your social qualifications and your contacts with others having similar qualifications. These alliances have a supportive function and may operate at personal, social and professional levels according to the level of 10th house accomplishments. At the personal level, we are seeing new forms of alliances. The new generation accepts the fact of two people (of either the same or opposite sex) living together in an unbonded relationship (often confused with a 7th house relationship). This kind of relationship implies total freedom along with cooperation and detached love. This is an ideal which is seldom reached, but also a goal through which we strive to enter the Aquarian Age. Society is not yet ready to accept such a radical expansion of 7th house relationships, partly because the new generation has not yet learned to handle them with the Aquarian detachment necessary for equality. Also, due to the balsamic nature of our transitional stage between two ages, no structures have yet been provided, and the new ideal is operating in the old Piscean structure.

At the professional level, the 11th house describes the resources needed to sustain your business, your image, your social responsibilities. These can be material, mental, emotional or psychological resources, the nature of which will be described by the sign on the cusp. The ruler of the 11th house shows how and where you sustain or maintain your 10th house position and image. Your personal value to society is shown by the 10th house and its ruler, but to maintain that value you must assert the type of energy shown by the planetary ruler of the 11th house, in the area of life described by its house position.

While the 2nd house will show the personal income drawn from your business, the 11th house shows the business' earning capacity—its capacity to gross sufficient funds to continually improve and update the operation. If you are not in business for yourself, this refers to your potential to improve and expand your social worth and thus maintain your social or organizational connections. Psychologically, the 11th house is your emotional capacity to sustain all struggles for achievement and for contribution through the inspiration of humanitarian ideals.

21.
Pisces, Neptune, & the 12th House

Pisces is the sign of universal love. Human love begins in Cancer at the most personal level, as love of mother or family or whatever makes you feel loved. It is a love that brings personal security, or fills your need to give others security. In Scorpio, your ability to love becomes transformed through the sacrifice of your own self-centeredness. This is still a personal love for another person or persons, but it is also a mature love in which one is not dependent on another for survival. Each contributes his share to the relationship. That is, this is the true significance of Scorpio. A negative Scorpio is working a relationship for all it is worth to get something out of it for himself.

If the Cancer love was too clinging and productive of no personal growth and maturity, then Scorpio's sting of death takes away the object of that love. In that case, Pisces can bring the complete dissolution of one's foundations. Or, the regenerative power of Scorpio may, through its "dark night" experience, generate the seed of possible new life in Pisces, the "seed" sign. Pisces then becomes universal love, no longer limited to the particular individual, nor to the motivation of personal emotion. This kind of love can fall equally on all people, including and especially, those rejected by society. Such an all-encompassing experience of love enables one to have faith in others, in humanity, or in God, to the extent of more or less total commitment to whatever giving seems to be required.

At the same time, this complete openness to all levels of humanity leaves the inexperienced Pisces (with an undeveloped Saturn) wide open to illusory and deceptive influences from those whose motives are less than pure. Being so open allows you to take into yourself and make a part of yourself anything within your sphere of activity. One of the key-words of Pisces is detachment. The major lesson is to understand with compassion but to refuse to accept the negative at the emotional level or become personally involved with it.

Cancer represents stored past memories which are the foundation of the personality. Scorpio represents deeper memories, containing potent psychological energies which have not all been integrated into the personality at its present level. In Pisces there are still other unconscious memories containing the distillation of the wisdom gained from the Cancer and Scorpio experiences. This is not philosophical or religious knowledge. It is more an inner truth from beyond the purely conscious levels. The characteristic of this knowledge is its universal quality—the fact that other people ultimately have come to the same conclusions.

This possession of ultimate truth, however partial, is the basis for the Pisces openness to others. You feel, without knowing why, that you "have been there," and in the same way, you respond to the essence of great poetry, music, art, and acts of unselfish dimension. Negative or positive, you "understand" it. The house occupied by Pisces shows an activity or area in which you are "karmically" required to give of this essence of distilled wisdom through the love it makes possible. This is a self-sacrificing love because you cannot expect anything in return. However, there seems to be a law of cause and effect that says love given always brings more back—"like attracts like."

Everyone has seen the picture of Jesus standing at the door, waiting for someone to open it because there is no knob on his side. Pisces is your door to the larger life, but the Sun is *you. You* have to make the effort, consciously. There are obviously many cases of genius, psychism, musical and mathematical talent, etc., in which the super-conscious is active on a daily level, as an intrusion into the personal conscious, but conscious effort was not involved. They were "invaded," and their present consciousness cannot integrate the higher content into total personality awareness, so it becomes highly unstable. These individuals often identify their ego with their super-normal accomplishments. You have heard the statement that all geniuses "are a little weird." In actuality, they are not fully integrated personalities and will not be until their daily level of consciousness is made to operate consistently on the level of their higher selves. In spite of appearances, gifted people are not always fortunate beyond the usual lot in life. It should be emphatically stated that the higher the level of evolution, the more difficult the decisions, the heavier the responsibilities, the greater the losses and the more one has to give up at the personal level. In short—a real Pisces trip.

The need of Pisces is to dissolve old ego-crystallizations built in the previous signs. These crystallizations of separateness that were formed through fear of losing that separateness are described in the Capricorn chapter. The accumulated love-wisdom of Pisces wants to dissolve the fear involved in hanging on to them and to overcome the separateness. Therefore, in the house of Pisces a commitment to the future, however uncertain, frightening and ego-dissolving, is required by the higher self. At the same time, it offers the faith to face the unknown activated by the Neptune experience.

There is no material reward in making this break from the past, and many people cannot see the significance in doing so. In many ways, the demand of the Pisces house really seems frightening psychologically, if not in other ways. Therefore, Pisces is a sign associated with escapism. This is only a negative reaction made by those who are not attuned to the vibration. For example: with Pisces on the 4th house, you might feel confined to your home for a period of time. You could waste that time, feeling sorry for yourself, or you could get more closely in touch with your own center. All Pisces-4th house individuals have to build their foundations on a deeper level than that which was given them by family, background and culture.

Even though, at one level, Pisces brings the most excruciating sense of confinement, when one finally gets hold of the key to its full reality, there is no longer any way one can ever be confined or dependent again. Pisces can expand into the universe from the smallest closet.

NEPTUNE ("the universal solvent") is the key to this expansion, showing the crystallizations that need to be dissolved in order to make the necessary commitment in Pisces. Neptune is the unconscious urge to transcend the attitudes and qualities represented by the sign it occupies. These are attitudes held toward the experiences of the house it occupies, and they always contain some old ego-crystallizations that need to be dissolved. For example, Neptune in the 7th house:

Old egocentric attitudes of intellectual superiority are being dissolved through partnerships. If responding negatively to Neptune, the subject will be caught up in illusions about his intellectuality, which the partner will continually and subtly dissolve. Often such a person unconsciously attracts partners with physical or psychological problems, in order to serve, save or sacrifice for them. Instead of dissolving the ego, it places them in a place of superiority! Under positive conditions, the urge to dissolve ego boundaries through relationships becomes a "like attracts like" situation in which love is given with no personal need for return and is received as an opportunity for spiritual growth.

In the house of Neptune you often find yourself involved in illusion and have trouble in distinguishing between it and reality. At the same time there is also a deep sense of obligation. You may feel pressure to lose yourself in the experience of the house. This does not mean loss of conscious control, but rather the need to lose the ego-centeredness of the sign-

attitudes. Illusion can cause you to allow something to literally swallow you up in order to live out some falsely based ideal, when you should be using your Virgo-polarity of discrimination. Pisces should be teaching you about the greater realities and making you a part of them.

Achieving some measure of this larger consciousness puts you in touch with the Pisces superconscious mind and its stored universal truths. This is the source of all true creative imagination. In the Neptune house you will then see things in terms of the greater reality rather than a blown-up illusion. You bring this new consciousness back to the Pisces house to be used in service to your commitment.

Aspects to personal planets in the chart are important keys to the way you channel your creativity. Aspects to Venus suggest artistic or musical ability; to Mercury, literary or synthetic talents; to the Moon, caring and compassion; to the Sun, integration of spiritual consciousness and imagination into the personal purpose. Aspects to Mars suggest you are channeling your imagination through your actions and personal desires. However, a hard aspect from Neptune to a personal planet suggests that something connected with the planet is denied to you in order to make you search for it at another level.

NEPTUNE RETROGRADE shows circumstances or people who force you to get behind illusion and find a more solid reality. Somewhere in your past your ideals and faith were based on illusion, or perhaps you had none at all. Now you have to rebuild that foundation in higher reality. You may strip the veil from false religious ideas (9th house), false authority-images (10th house), false knowledge acquired in early education (3rd house), false material values (2nd house), etc. Since an already unconscious planet is even more unconscious when retrograde, the process is hard to define. Usually the material comes up through dreams, visions, etc., that is, while you are in an "unconscious" state such as sleep or trance. You usually do not have the direct contact with the Pisces material that is available when it is not retrograde. Also, the material often comes in the form of symbols, even when

Neptune is direct, so this further hides meaning. All of this is saying that it requires considerable effort and conscious will to integrate the experiences into the total self. The dream symbols *could* be a form of guidance for reaching a new foundation for ideals, but unless you are operating very positively and consciously, they will simply confuse the issue. Neptune rules psychic activity, and when retrograde, it could suggest trance mediumship or other forms of unconscious psychism, but it takes a well-integrated person to be able to handle this kind of expression. Squares from personal planets, especially the Moon, are warnings of the dangers of using psychic gifts indiscriminately.

ASPECTS TO THE OTHER PLANETS show how the collective knowledge or wisdom of the superconscious is affecting the other personality functions. For example:

Collective wisdom is shaping:

The Sun — your conscious purpose, expanding the consciousness through dissolving self-centeredness.

The Moon — your emotional responses, dissolving past habits and dependencies in order to build the "mother image" on a more collectively significant level.

Mercury — your personal attitudes and mental concepts, opening your awareness to what lies beyond fact.

Venus — your personal values and receptive urges, love-power, bringing relationships which enlarge values or dissolving meaningless relationships in order to find more spiritual ones.

Mars — your natural physical urges, transforming them to enable you to use the Mars-energy for more collective purposes.

Jupiter — your learned ethical attitudes and concept of God, dissolving them in order to enlarge them.

Saturn — the socially conditioned ego, dissolving it to extend its boundaries and make it less separative.

Uranus — the intuitive function, dissolving old rebellious activity and feeding the originality with inspiration.

THE TWELFTH HOUSE is where you build the inner strength to overcome all your limitations, sorrows, fears, and dependencies. These are limitations relating to all of the other eleven houses, but they show up in connection with the 12th house when they are ready to be overcome or transcended. This could be shown in the chart when rulers of various houses transit or progress through the 12th, or when a planet natally occupies the 12th. The sign on the 12th house cusp represents an attitude and need that must be transcended in some way. The ruler's position shows what experience is needed to do this. It also shows a function involved in all efforts at overcoming "karma." A person with the ruler of the 12th in only easy aspects will find this function helpful in all karmic problems.

The 12th house is where the personal has to adapt to the collective. Everything you have misused or not used in the previous eleven houses comes home to roost in the 12th. This is why it is called the house of self-undoing, sorrow, confinement, secret enemies and institutions. We have all taken from society at many levels, and everything we have taken has to be repaid. (In some cases, society may owe us!) Those who have taken selfishly or at the expense of others have a greater debt, and payment will be *taken*, while others may find this house gives them the satisfaction of giving to those less fortunate.

This is also the house of the search for ultimate truth, beauty and goodness through inner experience, where one finds oneness of soul with God or humanity. Negatively this could mean the oneness one finds in a mental institution or prison where everyone dresses alike, is treated alike and is forced to behave alike. Interestingly enough, a nun, a soldier, a nurse or a priest find a similar experience. These ways of life can imply a loss of identity whereas the positive 12th house expression is to be able to know your place in this larger scheme of things without losing your own self-consciousness.

The inmate of a mental hospital really has lost his identity. Many of these people had psychic sensitivity that opened them to more collective influences (Neptune) than they had developed ego-consciousness (Sun/Saturn) to sustain or integrate. Nuns and priests give up even their own names (identity) as well as much outer individuality, and many have a struggle at least once in their lives to remain aware of their own inner individuality, integrating it with the collective ideal in terms of personal commitment.

A person who has abused the laws is forced into similar situations in the prison system. If he has a strong ego, the experience *should* dissolve some of the self-centered egotism and separativeness by forcing him into a position where he *has* to see himself as one among many. If he has a weak ego, he probably committed his crime through collective influence as an over-compensation for a feeling of personal inadequacy. This situation *should* create more self-awareness either through sheer discomfort or through being forced to carry out responsibilities with others who are obviously no better than himself. For the person with a weak ego, a sense of self-worth as a part of the larger whole should be fostered. In view of these truths revealed by astrological meanings, it seems important for prison officials to consider these two basic types of people in their care, when planning their programs.

A nurse and doctor face similar anonymity. Nurses in their white uniforms conjure up collective images of the Florence Nightingale "healing angel" type, which obscures their real individuality. Doctors are seldom called by their names—"The doctor will see you now," "The doctor is not in," "The doctor will explain it to you." Doctors need strong self-consciousness to retain their personal commitment, and a large total consciousness to understand the patient's needs without becoming overly involved in them or "drowned" by them.

All of these examples graphically illustrate one basic law. In the 12th house, you are operating with society, against it, or you are lost in it. If you really want to be with it, you have to give as well as receive; you must balance and integrate the personal with the collective, and know what is yours and what is not yours. If Pisces is the wisdom stored from the past, the 12th house is where you give of that wisdom, thus making room in your cup for greater wisdom and illumination to flow in. The people of the 12th house—prisoners, doctors, priests, soldiers—are all wearing masks and are all contributing to the larger whole through mass activity, or are becoming a burden through society's evils. Even if you are in none of these roles, a part of you, too, belongs in the 12th house and Pisces. You have your problems, sorrows, limitations, which can make you realize that you are a part of humanity and want to help others who are also limited. When you find the deep commitment of the 12th house and Pisces, this will lead directly to the experience of being re-born in Aries. . .

22.

Aries — I Am Re-born

If you have survived the journey into the darkness of your own being to discover the "God within," and have dedicated yourself to the greater unknown, you have emerged with a new identity. You now have the knowledge and wisdom of all this past experience and can live out your Pluto role at the *conscious* level through your house of Aries. Your Aries identity is no longer the separative "I am." In a much deeper way than when you started, you have consciously become a part of the larger whole.

You built ego-boundaries with Saturn. You broke those open with Uranus. You allowed Neptune to dissolve them so that you might come to know the Pluto "God-seed." This seed becomes the new identity. Your re-born identity is open to new Aries ideas from a higher realm, which inspire you to take new action and find a new direction in the house ruled by this sign. All of this can lead to a whole new image being projected in the first house, a positive new inner image in the fourth house, a new image in relationships in the seventh house and a new social image in the tenth house—IF you allow the spiral principle to continue working between the signs and houses.

You are now ready to answer again the 12 questions asked
at the beginning of this volume. Your chart contains the
answers, but in order to live them out, you have to be in touch
with the Self who is asking the questions . . .

Who Are You?
(The Spiral of Life)

1. (♈) Do you know who you are?
2. (♉) On what do you base your self-worth?
3. (♊) Are you learning from your daily experiences?

* * * * *

4. (♋) If the answers to these three questions are "yes," then you should be able to build stable personal foundations and a solid self-image.
5. (♌) Are you expressing your emotions through creative activity?
6. (♍) Are you willing to make personal adjustments to the world outside yourself by applying your knowledge in a practical way?

* * * * *

7. (♎) If so, you should be able to relate well on an inter-personal level and work harmoniously within equalitarian relationships.
8. (♏) Are you willing to control personal ego-centered desires out of respect for others in your life?
9. (♐) Are you trying to expand your knowledge, seeking a larger understanding of life through your social experiences? Can you see the broader viewpoint?

* * * * *

10. (♑) If so, you should be able to build solid foundations through which to operate on a social level, or gain a social image.
11. (♒) Are you searching for social or group awareness through shared expression and humanitarian experiences?
12. (♓) Are you willing to commit yourself to what you believe even though it may call for personal sacrifice?

* * * * *

Then you are ready for a startling experience . . .
There's a new life coming!!

GUIDELINES
FOR CHART
INTERPRETATION

23.

The Elements & Qualities

At the beginning of interpretation, it is important to assess the balance between the elements. For instance, we can see whether the person has sufficient activated air signs to handle the material side of life, as well as sufficient earth to stabilize his mental and creative activity. Activated fire signs are important in encouraging goal-oriented activity, which balances the element of water. Too much water holds one in the past and drowns enthusiasm with fears and limitations. With too little, the compassion and underlying emotional structures may be inadequate to support the goal-oriented activities of the fire. One can balance fire with earth, air with water, fire with air, and earth with water in the same way.

Traditionally, the number 3 is the number of spirit. Dividing the twelve signs by three produces the four elements. The relationships (i.e., aspects) between the three signs in each element show your potential for living life creatively. Spiritual astrologers would say these aspects indicate your spiritual development, which acts as a sustainment for life. Trines and Grand Trines between planets in the same element show that your creativity and expressive ability are well developed. Out-of-element trines may operate just as strongly and creatively, but probably with more complexity.

The three *water signs* represent three levels of the *past*.

> CANCER — the recent past of memory.

> SCORPIO — the hidden deep past of the subconscious.

> PISCES — the accumulated and distilled values from all past experiences.

The three *fire signs* represent the *future* potential of the personality.

> ARIES — action leading to identity awareness.

> LEO — striving for personality expression.

> SAGITTARIUS — reaching for socialization of personality.

The three *earth signs* show productive resources of the personality in the *present*.

> TAURUS — resources of the self.

> VIRGO — useful application of resources.

> CAPRICORN — productive social application of resources.

The three *air signs* show the intellectual activity of the personality in the *present*.

> GEMINI — personal knowledge and ideas.

> LIBRA — shared knowledge and ideas.

> AQUARIUS — universal knowledge and ideas.

Combining Signs and Houses

Water signs (Cancer, Scorpio, Pisces) — the past
Fire signs (Aries, Leo, Sagittarius) — the future
Earth signs (Taurus, Virgo, Capricorn) — the present
Air signs (Gemini, Libra, Aquarius) — the present

Angular houses (1, 4, 7, 10) represent the present.
Succedent houses (2, 5, 8, 11) represent the future.
Cadent houses (3, 6, 9, 12) represent the past.

When you are dealing with the unconscious past (water signs), the future goals (fire signs), and the present abilities (earth signs) within the chart, and you begin to synthesize these by considering the house cusps they occupy, you immediately become aware of what appear to be contradictions. You find a sign representing the past on a house relating to the future (succedent). In fact, the signs which correspond to the houses in a natural chart are contradictions in themselves.

Remembering that the water signs represent the past, fire the future, and earth and air the present, consider the idea that the four angular houses, which are naturally ruled by signs of each element—1-fire (future), 4-water (past), 7-air (present), 10-earth (present)—are all said to represent the *present*. The same situation exists with the succedent houses of the future and the cadent houses of the past. In relating the houses to signs and their elements, we have, for example, the "Houses of Life" (1, 5, 9) which correspond to the fire signs:

1st house — *present* self-awareness (angular) affecting future identity (Aries).

5th house — *future* extension of yourself (succedent) affecting future goals for self-expression (Leo).

9th house — *past* philosophies or religious beliefs (cadent) affecting future understanding and aspirations (Sagittarius).

We hope we can clear up some of this confusion with the following material, introduced as food for thought and a new way of combining houses with signs, one that has been implicit in their relationship all along but never expressed. In the following section we provide a list of key-words for houses and signs which you can mix and match according to your own chart. You will see that the experiences of each house will be affected either by the present, past or future attitudes and needs. We have also noticed that these house/sign relationships yield interesting past-life content, and we encourage you to further expand on these key-phrases.

♈ Your need to build a future identity through initiating new activity is affecting . . .

♉ Your present need to be productive and build personal values is affecting . . .

♊ Your present need for knowledge and ability to use reason is affecting . . .

♋ Your need for emotional security and identity-sustainment based upon past experiences is affecting . . .

♌ Your potential for future ego-fulfillment through expression of your identity is affecting . . .

♍ Your present need for mental productivity is affecting . . .

♎ Your present need for harmonious interchange is affecting . . .

♏ Your unconscious desire power stimulating the urge for deep involvements based on the past is affecting . . .

(1) your present level of self-awareness.

(2) your future potential for building resources and more solid self-worth.

(3) your use of knowledge gained from past environmental contacts.

(4) your present emotional foundations or unconscious self-image.

(5) your future potential for self-reproduction through creative forms of release.

(6) your personal adjustments to the past through fulfilling routine responsibilities.

(7) your present personal relationships which call for cooperation.

(8) your potential for future ego-regeneration.

♐ Your need for future understanding and principles gained from broader contacts is affecting . . .

(9) your use of past philosophies and personal expansion.

♑ Your present need for a social identity and respect from society is affecting . . .

(10) your present social image and reputation.

♒ Your present need for social awareness through the ability to free yourself from structured attitudes is affecting . . .

(11) your future social alliances and satisfaction of life goals.

♓ Your openness to higher realities and soul memory based on the past is affecting . . .

(12) your ability to transcend the limitations or Karma from the past.

The Three Qualities

It is in the *qualities* of the signs and their corresponding houses that we see another example of the spiral at work. The number 4 is a Saturn number, the number of man, incarnation or the material world. Dividing the signs and houses by four produces the *cardinal, fixed* and *mutable* qualities, corresponding to the *angular, succedent* and *cadent* houses. Each sign has a need, which finds fulfillment through the experiences represented by the house in which it is placed. Fulfillment here leads to the further development of the signs' house positions in the natural chart.

CARDINAL SIGNS show your potential to know yourself. As mentioned in the "Digested Astrologer," Vol. I, the cardinal signs are involved with physical activity in the outside world, each sign on its own level. It is this activity which enables individuals to build their identity and therefore know themselves. ANGULAR HOUSES show *who* you are, as the signs occupying the angular houses describe the four basic "images" of the personality—conscious self-image (1st), unconscious self-image (4th), relative image (7th) and public image (10th). Therefore, we find:

ARIES — personal identity contributing to . . .
1st HOUSE — conscious self-image (how you see yourself).

CANCER — foundation of the identity contributing to . . .
4th HOUSE — unconscious self-image.

LIBRA — identity fulfillment contributing to . . .
7th HOUSE — relative image (how you see yourself in and through others).

CAPRICORN — social establishment of identity contributing to . . .
10th HOUSE — public image.

FIXED SIGNS show your potential to establish yourself through productive activity and getting results. They represent the product and sustainment of the cardinal signs. SUCCEDENT HOUSES show what you are according to your values. Therefore, we find:

TAURUS — productivity of the self contributing to . . .
2nd HOUSE — personal worth.

LEO — ego-consciousness contributing to . . .
5th HOUSE — personal creativity.

SCORPIO — joint productivity contributing to . . .
8th HOUSE — joint resources.

AQUARIUS — social awareness contributing to . . .
11th HOUSE — group activity.

MUTABLE SIGNS show your potential for adaptation to what is outside (cardinal) through understanding the previous cardinal and fixed signs. CADENT HOUSES show your level of self-adjustment through mental activity. Therefore, we find:

GEMINI — concrete knowledge and ideas contributing to . . .
3rd HOUSE — adjustment to environment.

VIRGO — useful application of knowledge contributing
   to . . .
6th HOUSE — adjustment to other individuals.

SAGITTARIUS — abstract knowledge contributing to . . .
9th HOUSE — adjustment to social relationships.

PISCES — universal wisdom contributing to . . .
12th HOUSE — adjustment to some still larger relationship
   (the collective, God, etc.).

24.

Hints for Interpretation

The HOUSES show areas of life experience and represent the cycles of selfhood enacted in the outer world. The SIGNS on the cusps of the houses indicate the qualities of those experiences, or their level of growth. In other words, the signs represent the psychological needs of, and attitudes toward, the experiences of the houses.

The RULING PLANETS point to other experiences of life, where you move out to fill the needs of the houses they rule. Therefore, the houses ruled by the planets are closely connected with the activities of the houses they occupy, as they seem to show the *purpose* of the activity.

The CUSPS of a house can be compared to a door. The conditions defined by the ruling planet are the key which will open the door. Through its experiences, shown by the sign, house and aspects, you are able to fulfill the need of the sign on the cusp.

The following steps in understanding each function of the personality (planets) should be considered when one asks the twelve basic questions about one's life.

1. HOUSE POSITION: The planet's position by house shows where its function is operating most strongly. The house describes the activity in which the function is most responsive, as well as indicating what is being developed or stimulated due to the planet's presence.

2. SIGN POSITION: The planet's sign position describes the qualities it is expressing and the underlying attitudes which characterize its action. It describes the psychological needs which must be fulfilled for efficient functioning.

3. HOUSE(S) RULED BY THE PLANET: The house(s) ruled by the planet indicate an area of life where the planet can find fulfillment for the activities and needs of the house it occupies. The planet is moving out to gain experience in the house it occupies in order to fill the needs of the house it rules.

   (NOTE: Planets ruling two signs will find fulfillment in two different areas of life and on two different levels, as described by the signs. For example: Mercury gathers information in the house it occupies according to the nature of its sign position and brings it back to the Gemini house. It also classifies this knowledge so that it can be applied in a practical manner in the Virgo house.)

4. DISPOSITORS: The dispositor (ruler of the SIGN the planet occupies) defines by house, sign and aspect the way in which the planet can express its sign qualities.

5. HOUSE RULER: The ruler of the house the planet occupies describes the physical boundaries within which the planet must operate. The planet is forced to work within the conditions described by the house ruler. For example, a Cancer Sun occupying the Gemini-ruled house has to develop emotions within an intellectual framework. If the house ruler, Mercury, were found in the 7th house, other people would play an important part in the fulfillment of the Sun's potential. In fact, the ability to work cooperatively with others on an intellectual level would be the determining factor in the fulfillment of emotional needs (Cancer).

6. STELLIUMS BY HOUSE: A grouping of planets in any given house shows an emphasis on that type of experience. The activities of the house are necessary in order to fill the needs of the houses ruled by each planet.

7. STELLIUMS BY SIGN: A grouping of planets in one sign of the zodiac emphasizes the need of the sign. The ruling planet takes on greater responsibility, as all of the stellium planets will be dependent in some way on its function to support their action. Therefore, if the ruling planet is favorably aspected while the occupant planets are under stress, the problems arising in the house may actually stem from another area of life, described by the occupant planets' own houses. A stressfully aspected ruler with well aspected planets occupying its house may show outside conditions contributing to its development. *But*, until the ruler begins to operate constructively, its function will be limiting the fulfillment sought in the houses ruled by the occupant planets.

8. PHASE RELATIONSHIPS BETWEEN PLANET AND RULER: The phase relationship between the planet and the ruling planet of the house it occupies shows how the planet is going to deal with the boundaries imposed by the ruler. If these two planets are in aspect, these experiences will be activated, and the aspect will show the ease or difficulty in expression.

9. PART OF EXPRESSION OF THE PLANET AND RULER OF THE HOUSE: The Part of Expression of the combined functions will show where the phase meaning is most strongly lived out. The sign in which it is found will indicate one's individual or unique way of expressing the purpose of the phase.

10. ASPECTS TO THE OTHER PLANETS: Aspects to or from the other planets indicate what other personality urges (planets) help, hinder or challenge the planet's action, and therefore where there is added energy operating. The type of energy is shown by the aspect. If in aspect to a faster moving planet, its function will be shaping the

urges and action of the faster planet. If in aspect to a slower moving planet, the slower planet will be doing the shaping to the others' expression and therefore will have a strong influence on its function.

Other Things to Consider

INTERCEPTED SIGNS: When you find an intercepted sign, you also find two consecutive houses with duplicated signs on the cusps (i.e., Sagittarius on the 11th and 12th houses and Gemini on the 5th and 6th, with Virgo and Pisces intercepted in the 2nd and 8th). Intercepted signs represent delayed expression of the quality described by the sign, and therefore lead to delayed fulfillment of the described need. The duplicated signs are usually emphasized due to unsolved problems from the past. The house with the lower degree indicates the problem from the past, while the house with the higher degree shows the way the problem is operating in the here and now. Since the house with the lower degree is in a 12th house relationship to the following house, awareness of the problem concerning the past is seldom present. It is not until the experiences of the two pairs of duplicated signs have been pursued, and their needs at least partially fulfilled, that the qualities of the intercepted signs unfold into more conscious expression.

RETROGRADE PLANETS: The actions of retrograde planets are often as backward as their apparent motion. Personal planets (Mercury through Saturn) rule two signs. We have found that in their normal direct motion, these planets function in a manner that parallels the progression from the earlier sign ruled to the later. Mercury gathers and communicates knowledge from varied experiences (Gemini), then analyzes the knowledge and makes it useful (Virgo). When Mercury is retrograde, the Virgo process of analysis and discrimination is experienced before the knowledge can be communicated in Gemini fashion. Because the person with retrograde Mercury takes all information inside and relates it to his own personal life, it often gets caught up in details.

This same concept seems to apply to the other personal planets, as well as to Pluto, due to Pluto's rulership over Scorpio and Aries. The retrograde planet takes on, or emphasizes, the quality of the later sign it rules—it has to learn the lesson of the later sign first. For instance, Mars retrograde represses desires (Scorpio) in order to re-build the desire nature. Venus retrograde often represses feelings in order to re-build personal values.

Never underestimate the power of a retrograde planet. Although the retrograde planets often signify difficult experiences in early life, they present an opportunity to build your own uniqueness with little outside influence affecting it. Since the personality function does not operate in a manner considered "normal" to others in the early environment, you are forced to go inside yourself and rebuild the foundations for a new type of expression which suits your own personality.

The dispositor of the retrograde planet will show some factor behind the repressed condition of the planet. Aspects show facets of the personality connected with the foundations that you are building. Hard aspects (conjunctions, squares and oppositions) from the slower planets to the retrograde planet show other personality functions forcing the planet to re-evaluate. Easy aspects show other functions supporting the process. An aspect to the ruler of the house that is occupied by the retrograde planet shows the ease or difficulty in building foundations. An aspect to the dispositor of the retrograde planet will show ease or difficulty in developing the new level of expression of the sign quality. Like intercepted signs, retrograde planets are delayed in reaching full conscious expression. The process of internalization and re-building of the foundations allow the expression to emerge later in a fully "individualized" way.

MUTUAL RECEPTION: When two planets are in mutual reception (for example: Moon in Gemini and Mercury in Cancer), each wants to fulfill its need through the activities of the planet occupying its own sign, with which it is in mutual reception. There is a double stimulus at work with planets in this relationship. They work equally to fulfill the needs of each other's houses, creating a great deal of potential.

THE FINAL DISPOSITOR of a chart is a planet that ultimately disposes of most or all the other planets. It will do this through the planets in its own sign as these planets in turn dispose of still other planets and so on. (For example: Moon in Libra disposed by Venus in Aries disposed by Mars in Capricorn, etc.) In some charts, one planet can in this way dispose of all others. In other charts there will be three or four groupings of dispositors and their planets. A planet which disposes all or nearly all the others will probably wield a comparably greater influence on the personality. For detailed information on finding the dispositor and different patterns of dispositorship we recommend Thyrza Escobar's book, *Essentials of Natal Interpretation.*

Appendix

An Outline for Interpretation

I.   What general patterns do you find in the chart?
     A.   What is the visual pattern (bucket, hemispheric, etc.)?
     B.   Is there a hemisphere emphasis?
     C.   Are all planets in signs Aries to Libra?
     D.   Are all planets in signs Libra to Aries?
     E.   How are the qualities and elements represented?

        (For A to D see *The Digested Astrologer*, Vol. I.)

II.   SUN — self-consciousness and the need to "shine."
     A.   Where is the consciousness shaped? (house)
     B.   What qualities does it express? (sign)
     C.   What helps or hinders or challenges it? (aspects)
     D.   What controls its development? (dispositor)
     E.   Where does it seek fulfillment? (Leo)

III.   MOON — Emotions and responses based on the past.
     A.   Where are you most sensitive and responsive due to your early relationship with your mother? (house)
     B.   Describe the emotional responses and habit patterns. (sign)
     C.   What factors affect your responses? (aspects)

D. What controls your responses? (dispositor)

E. Where do your emotions seek fulfillment or security?
    (Cancer)

IV.   THE MOON'S NODES — Two opposite areas showing tension as
      a result of the activity of the Moon and Sun together, until they
      are integrated.

      A. Where is an activity where you can take something into your-
          self to enlarge personal consciousness? (north node)

      B. Where is an activity where you can give the results of the
          North Node activity to society, but where you can be
          drained if not taking in at the N. N.? (south node)

V.   ASCENDANT — Your approach to life and your self-awareness.

      A. What basic attitudes are you developing toward life? (sign)

      B. What experiences help bring these attitudes out? (ruler's
          house)

      C. What things in life are based on self-awareness? (aspects)

VI.   PARTS OF FORTUNE AND SPIRIT — Where does the above
      personality combination (Sun, Moon, and Ascendant) seek happi-
      ness and expression? (Part of Fortune) What implicit values
      subtly qualify this search? (Part of Spirit)

VII. MERCURY — Ability to learn, communicate, analyze and make
      knowledge useful.

      A. Where is your mind shaped? (house)

      B. How do you learn, etc.? (sign)

      C. For what purpose are you gaining knowledge and communi-
          cating it? (Gemini)

      D. Where do you put knowledge to practical use? (Virgo)

      E. What personality factor controls your mental activity?
          (dispositor)

      F. What factors affect it? (aspects)

VIII. JUPITER — The urge to associate beyond family and personal
      relationships in order to form principles for social living.

      A. Where do these associations center? (house)

      B. What are your attitudes and needs in associations? (sign)

      C. What helps or hinders or challenges your ability to expand
          through associations? (aspects)

      D. What factor controls the process? (dispositor)

      E. Where will you use your social values in increasing your
          understanding and widening horizons? (Sagittarius)

      F. Where will this contribute to your losing yourself in the
          larger whole? (Pisces)

IX. MERCURY/JUPITER PHASE — How you operate as a social being. The Part of Expression shows where.

X. MARS — The urge to act on the basis of personal desire.
   A. Where does desire most strongly stimulate you to take action? (house)
   B. What characterizes your ability to initiate action? (sign)
   C. What factors affect your actions and how? (aspects)
   D. What factor controls your actions? (dispositor)
   E. Where do your energy-drives seek personal fulfillment? (Aries)
   F. Where do your energy-drives seek joint or group fulfillment? (Scorpio)

XI. VENUS — The ability to attract and appreciate people and things.
   A. In what area of life are you building material and personal values? What or whom do you attract? (house)
   B. What is your attitude toward love? (sign)
   C. What helps or hinders your capacity to love? (aspects)
   D. What controls it? (dispositor)
   E. Where will this ability find fulfillment in material enjoyment? (Taurus)
   F. Where will it find fulfillment in relationships? (Libra)

XII. MARS/VENUS PHASE — How your desire/value nature functions. The Part of Expression shows where your creative energies function most naturally.

XIII. SATURN — Your ability to find a place in society.
   A. Where do limitations and responsibilities defined by your father-relationship show that you need to build foundations for operating in society? (house)
   B. How do you go about building social foundations? (sign)
   C. What factors help or hinder the process? (aspects)
   D. What factor controls your response to your father's example? (dispositor)
   E. Where does your ambition to gain respect find fulfillment? (Capricorn)
   F. Where does it want to become more universal? (Aquarius)

XIV. SATURN/MOON PHASE — Conscious ego activity. SATURN/JUPITER PHASE — Social stability. SATURN/URANUS PHASE — Social creativity.

XV.   URANUS — The urge toward awareness of universal forces be-
      hind your conditioned personality.
      A.   What sudden changes or interruptions bring this awareness?
           (house)
      B.   What kind of awareness does it bring? (sign)
      C.   What factors help or challenge expression of your inner
           creativity? (aspects)
      D.   What controls its expression? (dispositor)
      E.   Where does this inner person or High Self seek fulfillment
           through getting you to break out of old patterns and accept
           new, more universal knowledge? (Aquarius)

XVI. NEPTUNE — The urge to lose yourself in some larger whole.
      A.   Where do you dissolve ego-boundaries to do this? (house)
      B.   What attitudes need to be transcended? (sign)
      C.   What factors help or hinder? (aspects)
      D.   What factor controls this process? (dispositor)
      E.   Where does the urge find fulfillment in compassion, inner
           strength, commitment or imagination? (Pisces)

XVII. PLUTO — The unconscious compulsion to become *totally* in-
      volved in something outside yourself.
      A.   Where do complexes or blocks prevent involvement, or in-
           dicate hidden energies seeking release in social activities?
           (house)
      B.   What kind of personality attitudes need transforming? (sign)
      C.   What factors help or challenge the process? (aspects)
      D.   What factor controls the process? (dispositor)
      E.   Where does total involvement work out in your life?
           (Scorpio)
      F.   Where do you find a new identity as a result? (Aries)

STUDY COURSES ON TAPE
by Joanne Wickenburg

TOWARD GREATER CONSCIOUSNESS is a taped study course on psychological interpretation of the horoscope, geared to GROUP interaction. Not only does it help hold a study group together, but it is an especially useful tool for beginning teachers, or for those advanced teachers who are starting to work with the psychological approach to astrology. If you wish to start a group without a teacher, the material provides the content, organization, structure and discussion guides needed for maintaining intellectual stimulation and quality of group participation.

THE TAPES: Six one-hour tapes contain material for 12 sessions.

THE STUDY GUIDE: Each participant will need the 70-page Study Guide that supplements the tapes. The Study Guide includes illustrations, evaluation sheets, example charts, etc. A complimentary copy of *Your Cosmic Mirror* (the supplement to *The Spiral of Life*) is included with each Study Guide.

THE FEE: One set of six tapes with a Study Guide, *Your Cosmic Mirror,* and a set of moderator sheets for the organizer of the group.
. . . . $50.00

Individual Study Guides for the group members, plus *Your Cosmic Mirror* . . . . $ 5.95

The Spiral of Life is the only book required for the course, outside of the Study Guide. Each person will need one . . . . $ 7.95

ORDER THROUGH: SEARCH
                         P. O. Box 162, Northgate Station
                         Seattle, Washington 98125

FOR THE INDIVIDUAL WORKING ALONE . . .

Joanne Wickenburg has designed a complete correspondence course in astrology entitled, *Astrology, the Cosmic Pattern.* Courses are available at all levels — from beginning through advanced. For more information on the course, write to the above address.

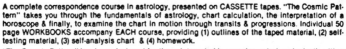

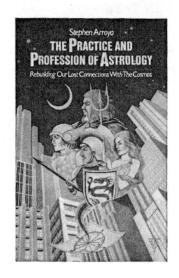

IMPORTANT BOOKS FROM CRCS

CRCS PUBLICATIONS

CRCS PUBLICATIONS publishes high quality books that focus upon the modernization and formulation of astrology. We specialize in pioneering works dealing with astrological psychology and the synthesis of astrology with counseling and the healing arts. CRCS books utilize the insights of astrology in a practical, constructive way as a tool for self-knowledge and increased awareness.

ASTROLOGY, PSYCHOLOGY & THE FOUR ELEMENTS: An Energy Approach to Astrology & Its Use in the Counseling Arts by Stephen Arroyo
.... $7.95 Paperback; $14.95 Hardcover
An international best-seller, this book deals with the relation of astrology to modern psychology and with the use of astrology as a practical method of understanding one's attunement to universal forces. Clearly shows how to approach astrology with a real understanding of the energies involved. Awarded the British Astrological Assn's. Astrology Prize. A classic translated into 8 languages!

ASTROLOGY AND THE MODERN PSYCHE: An Astrologer Looks at Depth Psychology by Dane Rudhyar .... 182 pages, Paperback $5.95
Deals with Depth-Psychology's pioneers with special emphasis on Jung's concepts related to astrology. Chapters on: Psychodrama, Psychosynthesis, Sex Factors in Personality, the Astrologer's Role as Consultant.

ASTROLOGY, KARMA, & TRANSFORMATION: The Inner Dimensions of the Birth-Chart by Stephen Arroyo .... 264 pages, $9.95 Paperback; $17.95 Deluxe Sewn Hardcover
An insightful book on the use of astrology as a tool for spiritual and psychological growth, seen in the light of the theory of karma and the urge toward self-transformation. International best-seller.

CYCLES OF BECOMING: The Planetary Pattern of Growth by Alexander Ruperti
.... 6 x 9 Paperback, 274 pages, $9.95
The first complete treatment of transits from a humanistic and holistic perspective. All important planetary cycles are correlated with the essential phases of psychological development. A pioneering work!

AN ASTROLOGICAL GUIDE TO SELF-AWARENESS by Donna Cunningham, M.S.W.
.... 210 pages, Paperback $6.95
Written in a lively style by a social worker who uses astrology in counseling, this book includes chapters on transits, houses, interpreting aspects, etc. A popular book translated into 3 languages.

RELATIONSHIPS & LIFE CYCLES: Modern Dimensions of Astrology by Stephen Arroyo
.... 228 pages, Paperback $7.95
A collection of articles and workshops on: natal chart indicators of one's capacity and need for relationship; techniques of chart comparison; using transits practically; counseling; and the use of the houses in chart comparison.

REINCARNATION THROUGH THE ZODIAC by Joan Hodgson ..... Paperback $5.50
A study of the signs of the zodiac from a spiritual perspective, based upon the development of different phases of consciousness through reincarnation. First published in England as *Wisdom in the Stars*.

LOOKING AT ASTROLOGY by Liz Greene .... 8½ x 11, $5.95
A beautiful, full-color children's book for ages 6-13. Illustrated by the author, this is the best explanation of astrology for children and was highly recommended by *School Library Journal*. It emphasizes a healthy self-acceptance and a realistic understanding of others. A beautiful gift for children or for your local library.

A SPIRITUAL APPROACH TO ASTROLOGY by Myrna Lofthus ... Paperback $12.50
A complete astrology textbook from a karmic viewpoint, with an especially valuable 130-page section on karmic interpretations of all aspects, including the Ascendant & M.C. A huge 444-page, highly original work.

THE ASTROLOGER'S GUIDE TO COUNSELING: Astrology's Role in the Helping Professions by Bernard Rosenblum, M.D. .... Paperback $7.95
Establishes astrological counseling as a valid, valuable, and legitimate helping profession, which can also be beneficially used in conjunction with other therapeutic and healing arts.

THE JUPITER/SATURN CONFERENCE LECTURES *(Lectures on Modern Astrology Series)* by Stephen Arroyo & Liz Greene .... Paperback $8.95
Transcribed from lectures given under the 1981 Jupiter/Saturn Conjunction, talks included deal with myth, chart synthesis, relationships, & Jungian psychology related to astrology.

THE OUTER PLANETS & THEIR CYCLES: The Astrology of the Collective *(Lectures on Modern Astrology Series)* by Liz Greene .... Paperback $7.95
Deals with the individual's attunement to the outer planets as well as with significant historical and generational trends that correlate to these planetary cycles.

CHILD SIGNS: Understanding Your Child Through Astrology by Dodie & Allan Edmands
150 pages, 12 photos of children .... Paperback $6.95
An in-depth treatment of a child's developmental psychology from an astrological viewpoint. Recommended by *Library Journal*, this book helps parents understand and appreciate their children more fully. Nice gift!

DYNAMICS OF ASPECT ANALYSIS: New Perceptions in Astrology by Bil Tierney.
Groundbreaking new work! .... 288 pages, Paperback $8.95
The most in-depth treatment of aspects and aspect patterns available, including both major and minor configurations. Also includes retrogrades, unaspected planets & more!

ASTROLOGY FOR THE NEW AGE: An Intuitive Approach by Marcus Allen ....
.... Paperback $5.95
A highly original work with an uplifting quality. Emphasizes self-acceptance and tuning in to your own birth chart with a positive attitude. Helps one create his or her own interpretation. Ready now.

THE PRACTICE & PROFESSION OF ASTROLOGY: Rebuilding Our Lost Connections w the Cosmos by Stephen Arroyo .... late 1984, Paperback $7.
A challenging, often controversial treatment of astrology's place in modern society and of astrological counselin as both a legitimate profession and a healing process.

HEALTH-BUILDING: The Conscious Art of Living Well by Dr. Randolph Stone, D.C., D.
Approx. 150 pages, Paperback
A complete health regimen for people of all ages by an internationally renowned doctor who specialized in proble cases. Includes instructions for vegetarian/purifying diets and energizing exercises for vitality and beau Illustrated with drawings & photographs.

POLARITY THERAPY: The Complete Collected Works by the Founder of the System, D Randolph Stone, D.O., D.C. (In 2 volumes, 8½ x 11),
The original books on this revolutionary healing art available for the first time in trade editions. Fully illustrat with charts & diagrams. Sewn paperbacks, over 500 total pages.

A JOURNEY THROUGH THE BIRTH CHART: Using Astrology on Your Life Pat by Joanne Wickenburg...168 pages, Paperback $7.95
Gives the reader the tools to put the pieces of the birth chart together for self-understanding and encourages creative interpretation of charts by helping the reader to think through the endless combinations of astrological symbols. Clearly guides the reader like no other book.

THE ASTROLOGY OF SELF-DISCOVERY: An In-Depth Exploration of the Potentials Revealed in Your Birth Chart by Tracy Marks......
288 pages, Paperback................................$8.95
A guide for utilizing astrology to aid self-development, resolve inner conflicts, discover and fulfill one's life purpose, and realize one's potential. Emphasizes the Moon and its nodes, Neptune, Pluto, & the outer planet transits. An important & brilliantly original new work!

THE PLANETS & HUMAN BEHAVIOR by Jeff Mayo...180 pp, Paperback $7.95
A pioneering exploration of the symbolism of the planets, blending their modern psychological significance with their ancient mythological meanings. Includes many tips on interpretation!

ASTROLOGY IN MODERN LANGUAGE by Richard B. Vaughan...340 pp, $9.95
An in-depth interpretation of the birth chart focusing on the houses and their ruling planets-- including the Ascendant and its ruler. A unique, strikingly original work! (paperback)

THE ART OF CHART INTERPRETATION: A Step-by-Step Method of Analyzing, Synthesizing & Understanding the Birth Chart...by Tracy Marks Paperback $7.95
A guide to determining the most important features of a birth chart. A must for students!

THE SPIRAL OF LIFE: Unlocking Your Potential With Astrology..... by Joanne Wickenburg & Virginia Meyer...paperback.........$7.95
Covering all astrological factors, this book shows how understanding the birth pattern is an exciting path towards increased self-awareness and purposeful living.

HOW TO HANDLE YOUR T-SQUARE by Tracy Marks...(new edition)..$10.95
The meaning of the T-Square, its focal planets, aspects to the rest of the chart, and its effect in chart comparisons, transits and progressions. A perennial best seller! (paperback)

NUMBERS AS SYMBOLS OF SELF-DISCOVERY by Richard B. Vaughan......
336 pages, Paperback...............................$7.95
A how-to book on personal analysis & forcasting your future through Numerology. His examples include the number patterns of a thousand famous personalities.

For more complete information on our books, a complete booklist, or to order any of the above publications, WRITE TO:

CRCS PUBLICATIONS
Post Office Box 20850
Reno, Nevada 89515-U.S.A.